PIANO • VOCAL • GUITAR

FEEL GOOD SONGS

ISBN-13: 978-1-4234-1855-9
ISBN-10: 1-4234-1855-7

HAL•LEONARD®
CORPORATION
7777 W. BLUEMOUND RD. P.O. BOX 13819 MILWAUKEE, WI 53213

Visit Hal Leonard Online at
www.halleonard.com

ANGEL

Words and Music by
SARAH McLACHLAN

Original key: Db major. This edition has been transposed down one half-step to be more playable.

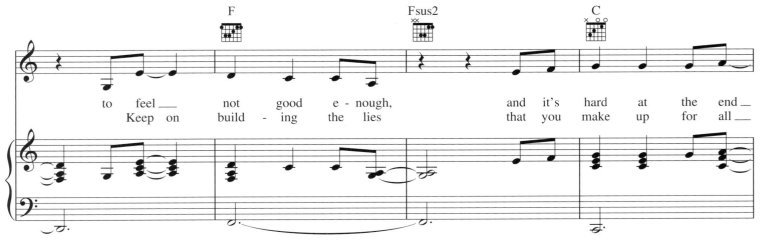

to feel ___ not good e - nough,
Keep on build - ing the lies

and it's hard at the end ___
that you make up for all ___

___ of the day. _____
___ that you lack. _____

I need some dis - trac - tion
It don't make no dif - f'rence

oh _____ beau - ti - ful re - lease. _____
es - cap - ing one last time. _____

Mem - o - ry
It's eas - i - er

seep from my ___ veins.
to be - lieve

Let me be emp - ty
in this sweet mad - ness,

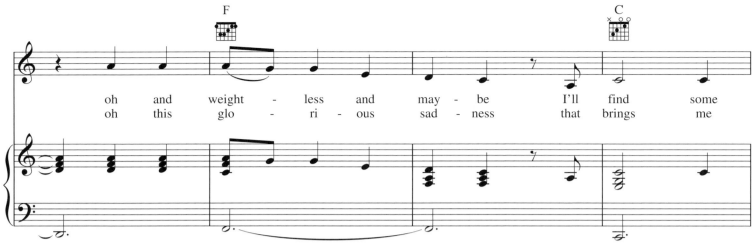

oh and weight - less and may - be I'll find some
oh this glo - ri - ous sad - ness that brings me

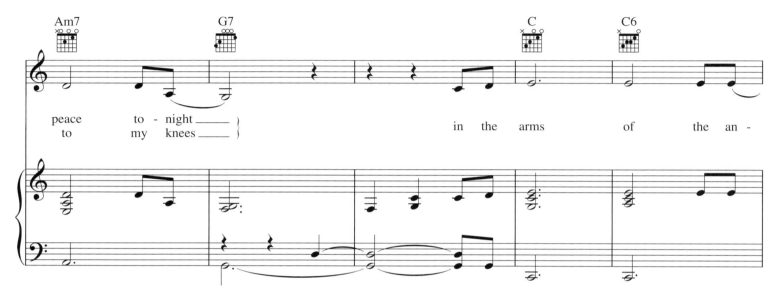

peace to - night _____ }
to my knees _____ }

in the arms of the an -

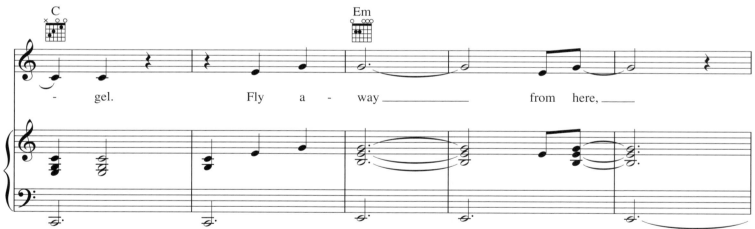

- gel. Fly a - way _____ from here, _____

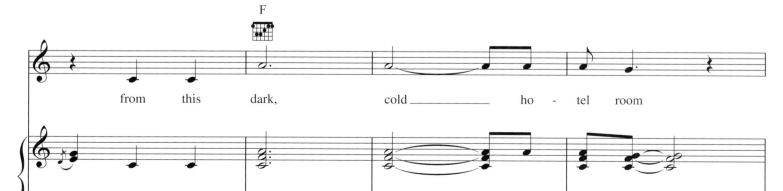

from this dark, cold _____ ho - tel room

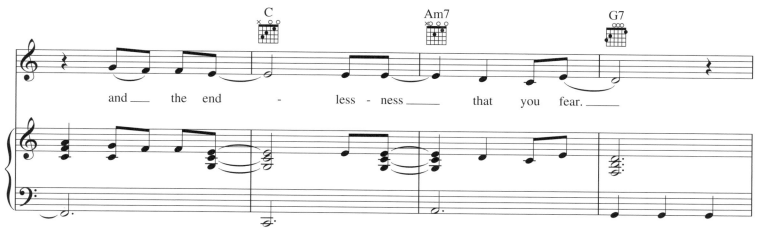

and ___ the end - less - ness ___ that you fear. ___

You are ___ pulled from ___ the wreck - age

of your si - lent ___ rev - er - ie. ___

You're in the arms of ___ the an - gel.

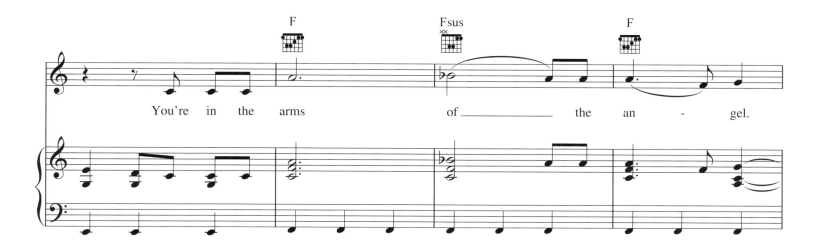

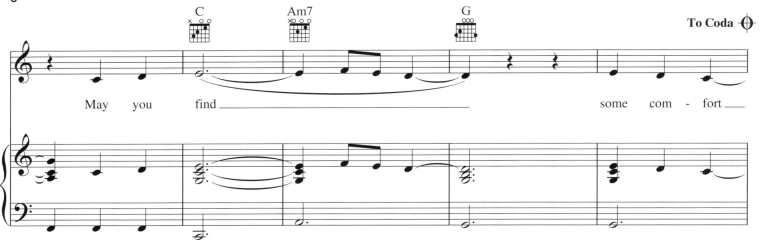

To Coda ⊕

May you find _____ some com - fort _____

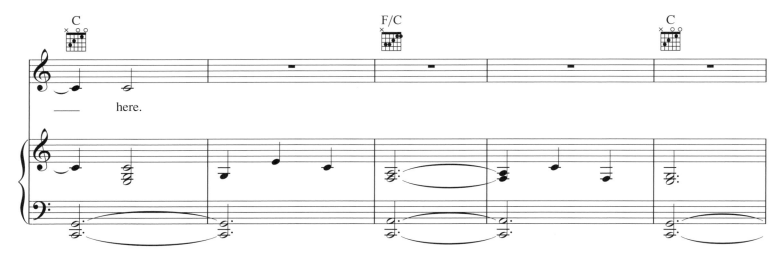

_____ here.

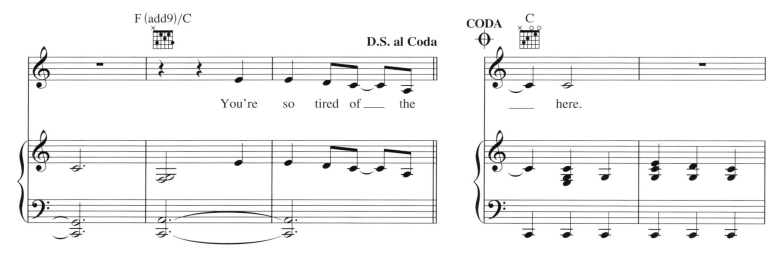

D.S. al Coda

You're so tired of ___ the

CODA ⊕

_____ here.

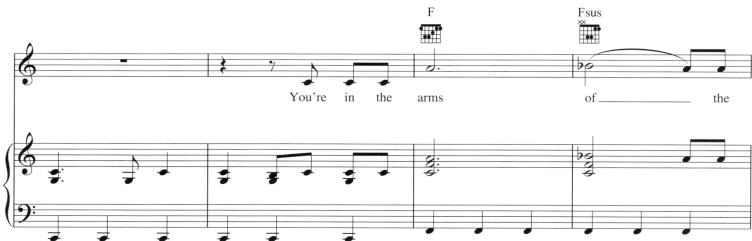

You're in the arms

of _____ the

an - gel. May you find

some com - fort here.

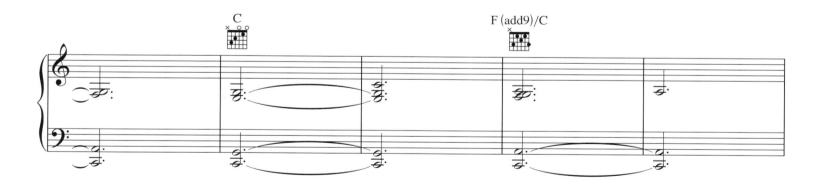

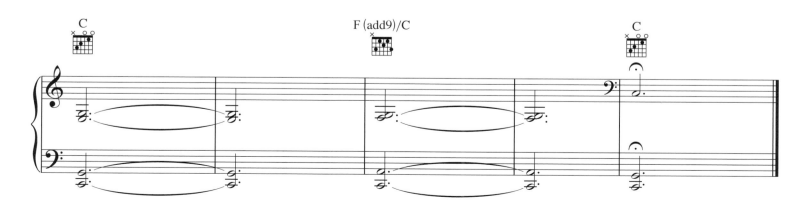

ANYTIME YOU NEED A FRIEND

Words and Music by MARIAH CAREY
and WALTER AFANASIEFF

and love will be ___ there _____ to light the way. ___
and love will be ___ there _____ to guide you home. ___

An - y - time you need a friend ___ I will be here. ___ You'll nev - er be a - lone a - gain ___

___ so, don't you fear. _____ E - ven if you're miles a - way, ___

___ I'm by your side. _____ So, don't you ev - er be lone - ly.

Love will make ___ it al - right. ___

___ If you just be - lieve ___ in me ___

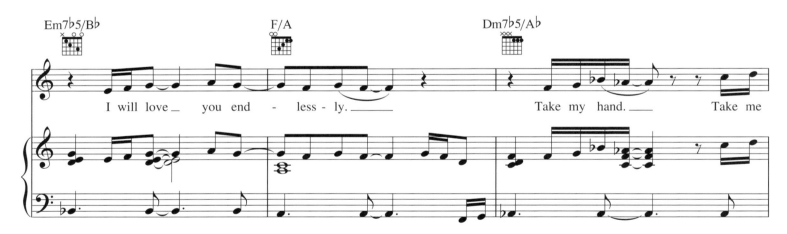

I will love ___ you end - less - ly. ___ Take my hand. ___ Take me

in - to your heart. ___ I'll be there ___ for - ev - er, ba - by. I won't let go. I'll nev - er let

go. _____ An-y-time you need a friend _____ I will be here. _

_____ You'll nev-er be a-lone a-gain _____ so, don't you fear. _

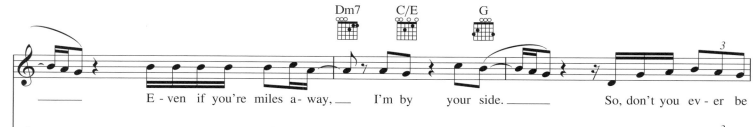

_____ E-ven if you're miles a-way, _ I'm by your side. _____ So, don't you ev-er be

Repeat and Fade

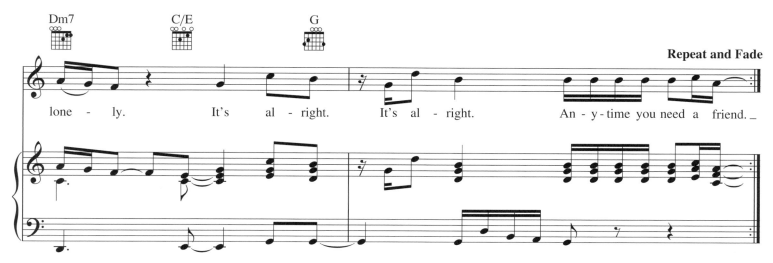

lone - ly. It's al - right. It's al - right. An - y-time you need a friend. _

BEAUTIFUL

Words and Music by
LINDA PERRY

Moderately slow

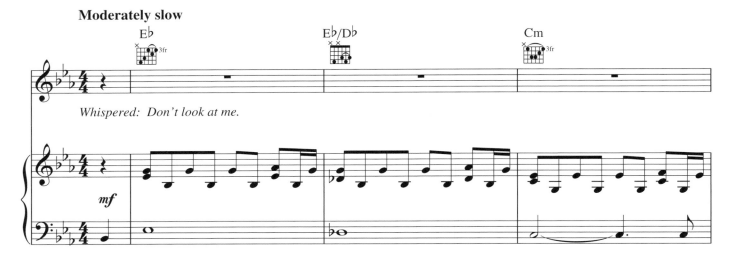

Whispered: Don't look at me.

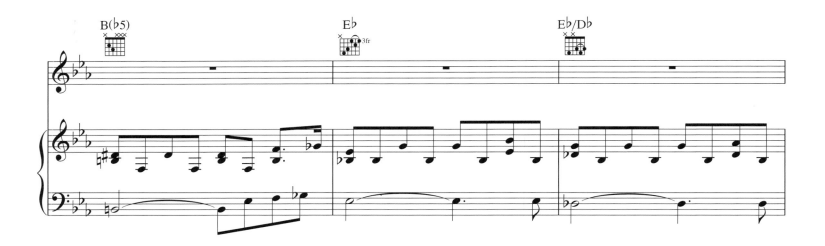

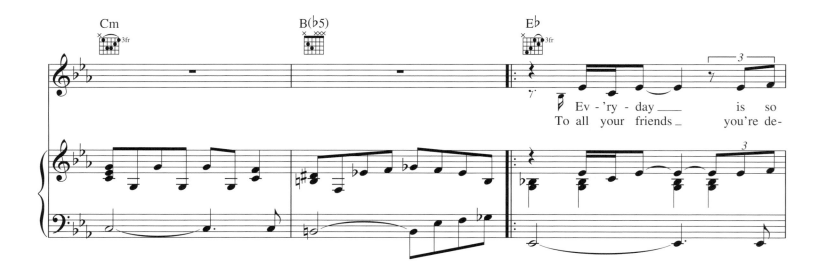

Ev - 'ry - day ___ is so
To all your friends ___ you're de-

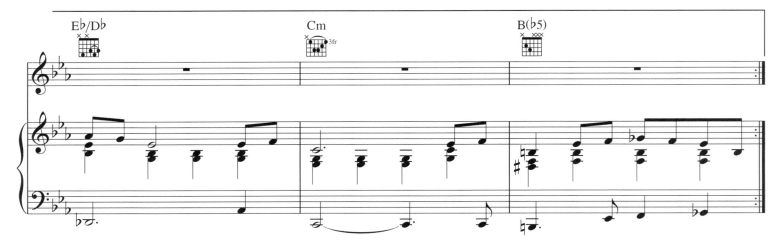

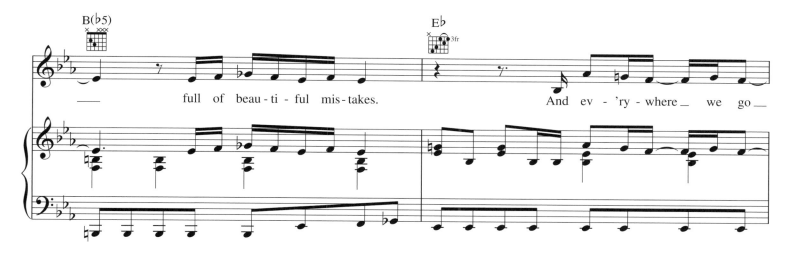

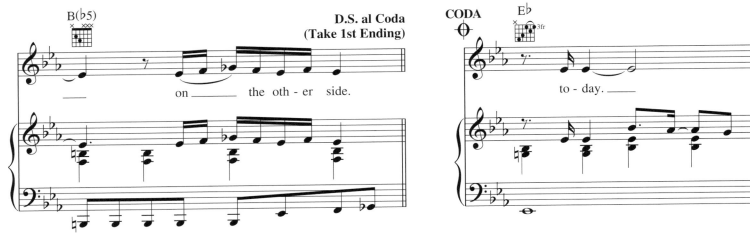

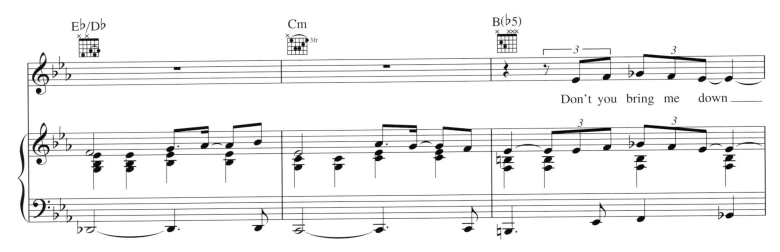

BLESS THE BROKEN ROAD

Words and Music by MARCUS HUMMON,
BOBBY BOYD and JEFF HANNA

Moderately

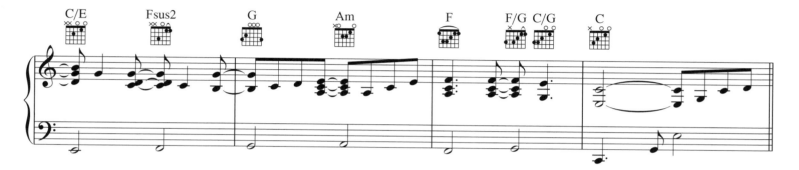

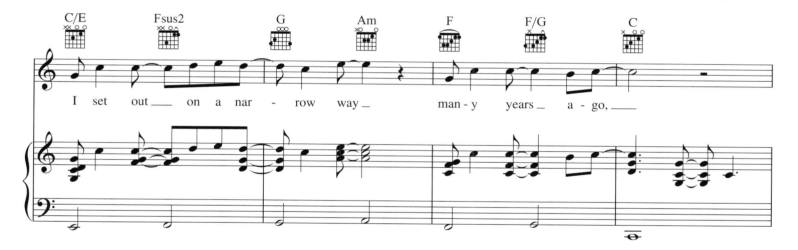

I got lost ___ a time ___ or ___ two, ___ wiped my brow ___ and kept push-in' through. ___

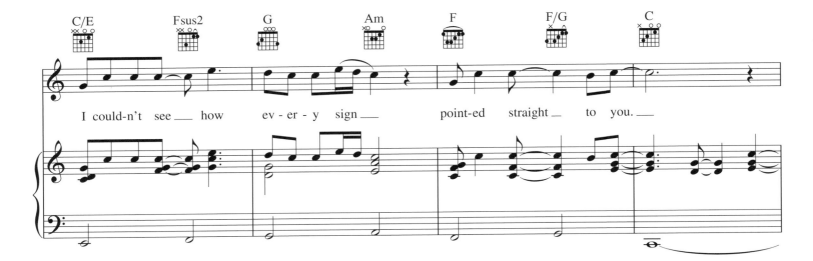

I could-n't see ___ how ev-er-y sign ___ point-ed straight ___ to you. ___

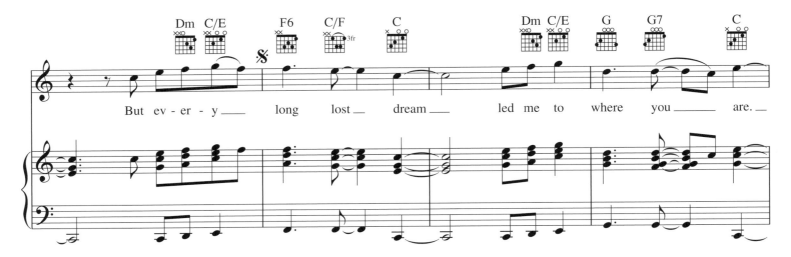

But ev-er-y ___ long lost ___ dream ___ led me to where you ___ are. ___

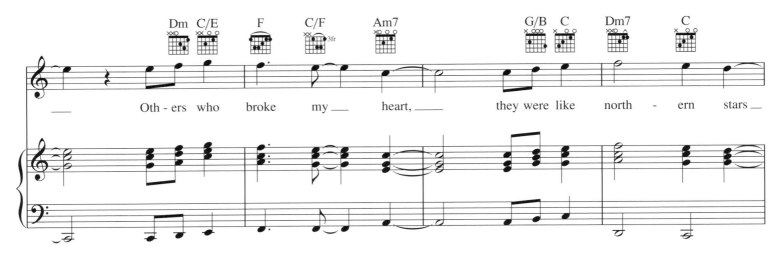

___ Oth-ers who broke my ___ heart, ___ they were like north-ern stars ___

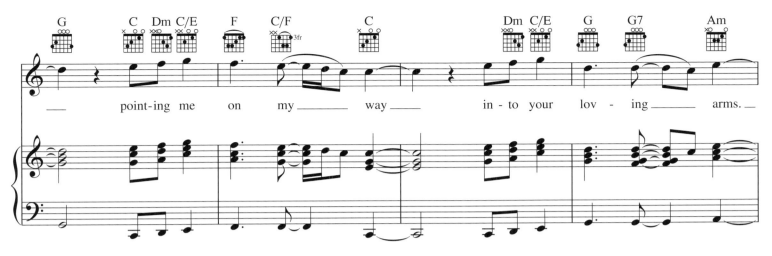

point-ing me on my _____ way _____ in-to your lov-ing _____ arms. ___

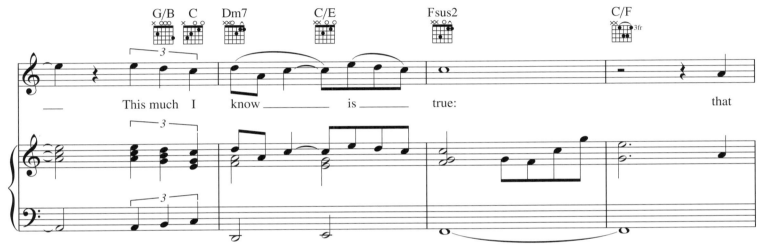

___ This much I know _____ is _____ true: that

God blessed _ the bro - ken road ____ that led me straight _ to you. _____

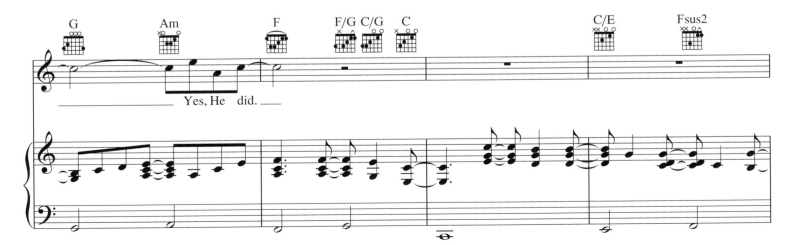

_____ Yes, He did. ____

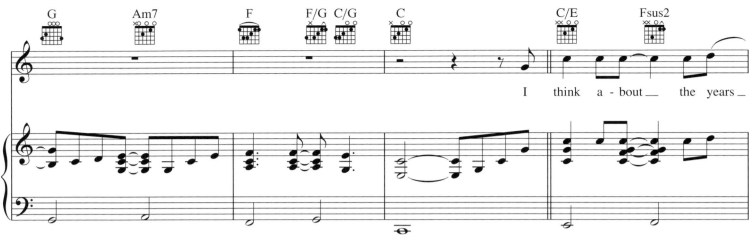

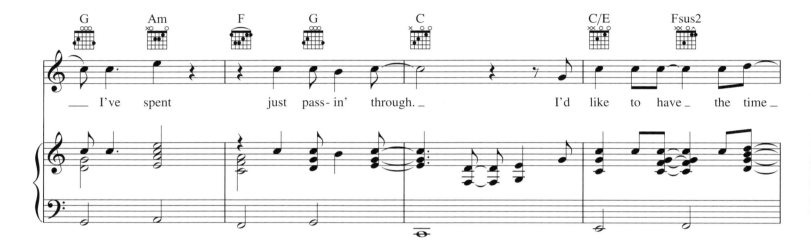

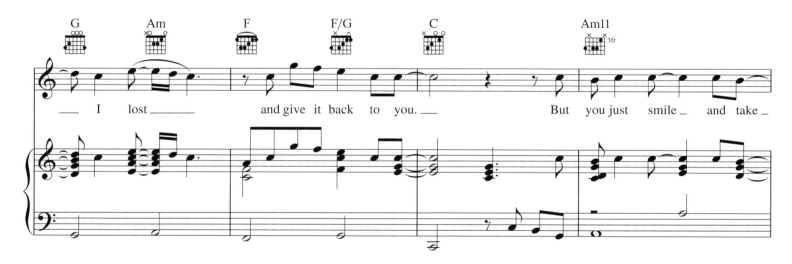

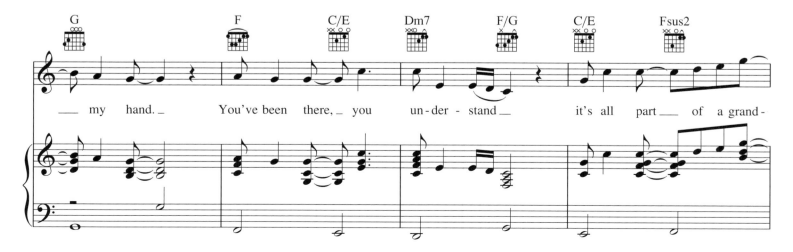

D.S. al Coda

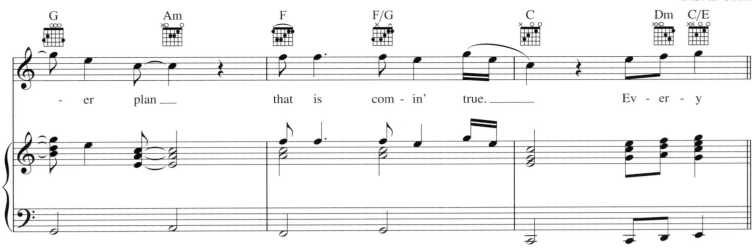

-er plan ___ that is com - in' true. _____ Ev - er - y

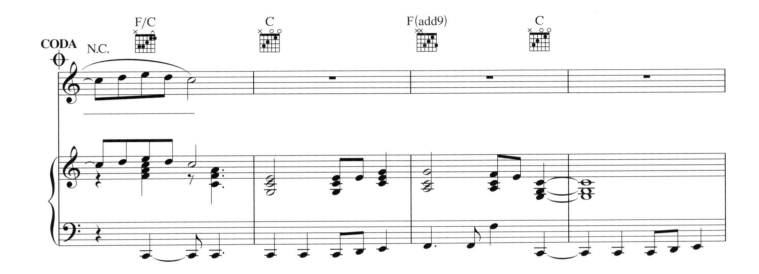

Now I'm just a - roll - in' ___ home _____

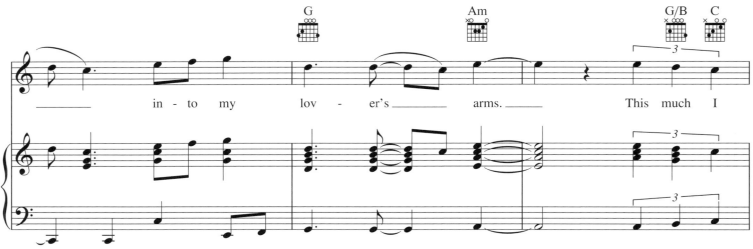

in - to my lov - er's _____ arms. _____ This much I

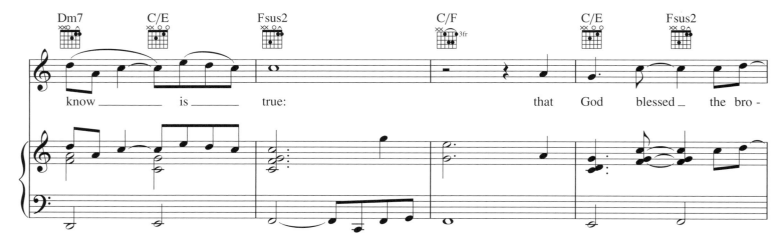

know _____ is _____ true: that God blessed _ the bro -

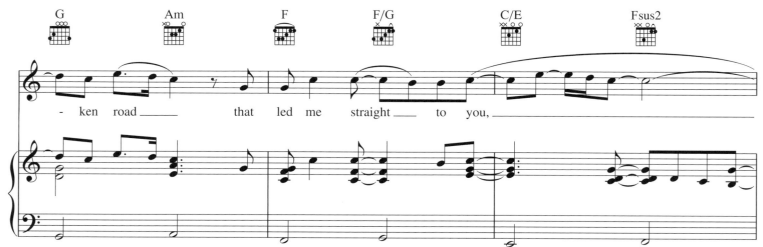

- ken road _____ that led me straight _____ to you, _____

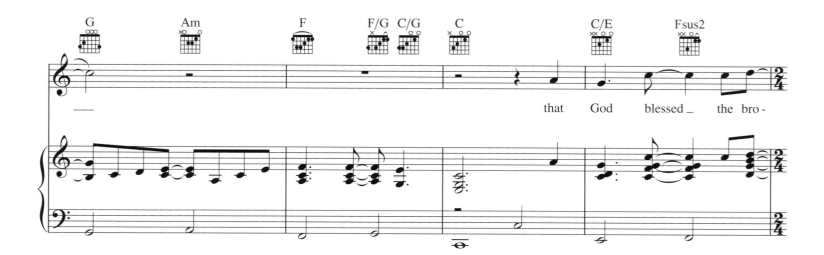

that God blessed _ the bro -

- ken road _____ that led me straight ___

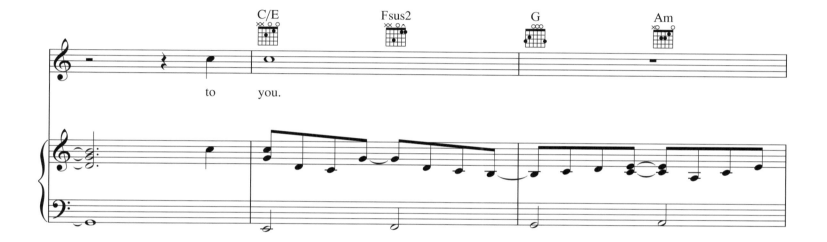

to you.

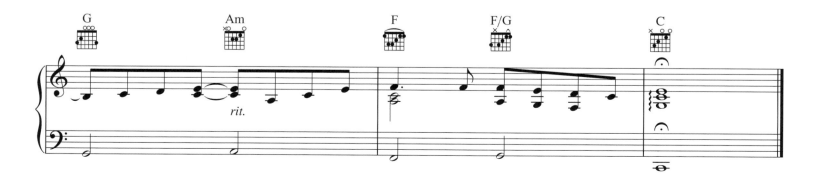

BUTTERFLY KISSES

Words and Music by BOB CARLISLE
and RANDY THOMAS

Smoothly

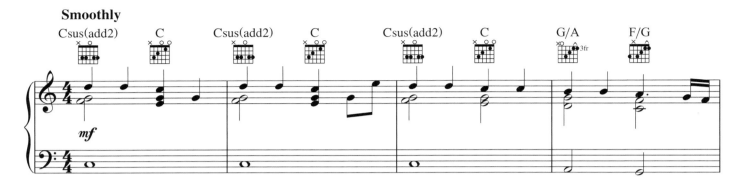

There's two things I know for sure. ___ She was
Sweet six - teen to - day, ___ she's
She'll change her name to - day. ___

sent here from heav - en and she's dad - dy's lit - tle girl. ___ As I
look - ing like her mom - ma a lit - tle more ev - 'ry day. ___
She'll make a prom - ise, and I'll give her ___ a - way. ___

drop to my knees ___ by her bed _____ at night, ___
One part wom - an, the oth - er part, girl. To
Stand - ing in the bride room just star - ing at her, she

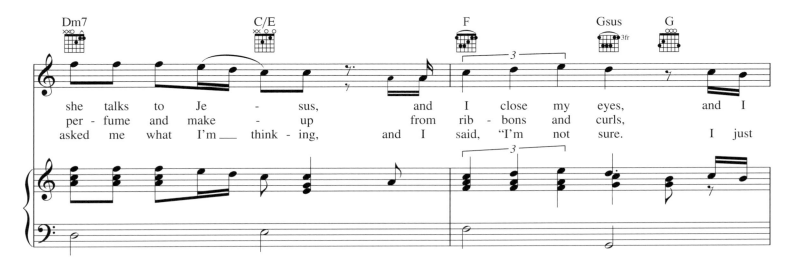

she talks to Je - sus, and I close my eyes, and I
per - fume and make - up from rib - bons and curls,
asked me what I'm ___ think - ing, and I said, "I'm not sure. I just

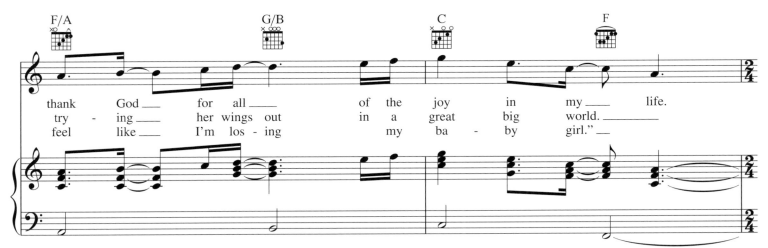

thank God ___ for all ___ of the joy in my ___ life.
try - ing ___ her wings out in a great big world. _____
feel like ___ I'm los - ing my ba - by girl." ___

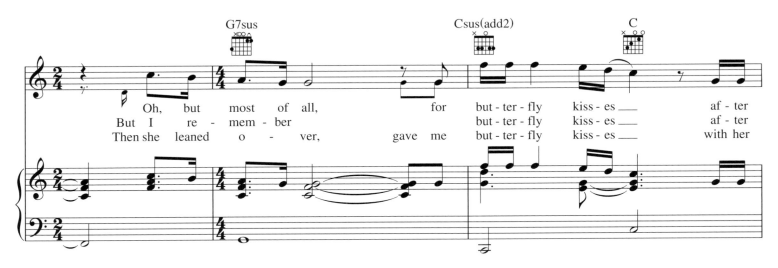

Oh, but most of all, for but - ter - fly kiss - es ___ af - ter
But I re - mem - ber but - ter - fly kiss - es ___ af - ter
Then she leaned o - ver, gave me but - ter - fly kiss - es ___ with her

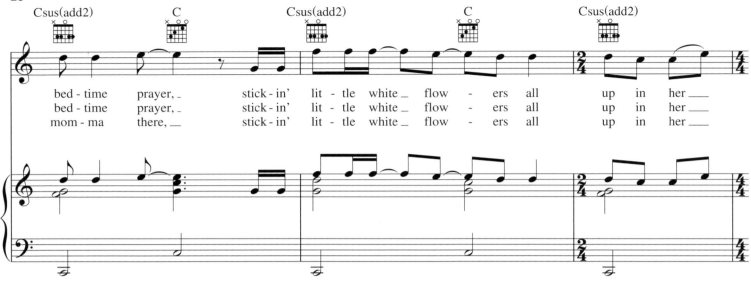

bed - time prayer, ___ stick - in' lit - tle white ___ flow - ers all up in her ___
bed - time prayer, ___ stick - in' lit - tle white ___ flow - ers all up in her ___
mom - ma there, ___ stick - in' lit - tle white ___ flow - ers all up in her ___

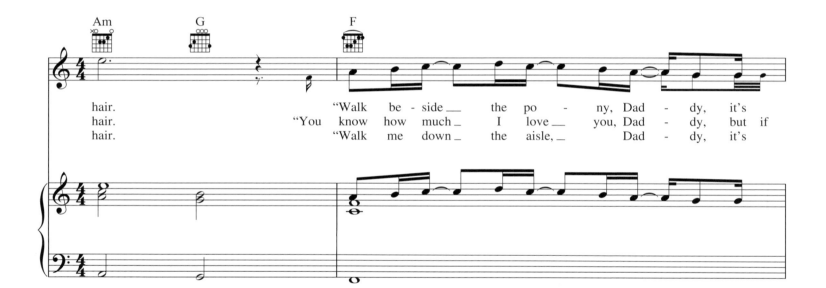

hair. "Walk be - side ___ the po - ny, Dad - dy, it's
hair. "You know how much ___ I love ___ you, Dad - dy, but if
hair. "Walk me down ___ the aisle, ___ Dad - dy, it's

my first ride. ___ I know the cake ___ looks fun - ny, Dad - dy, but
you don't mind, ___ I'm on - ly goin' ___ to kiss ___ you on ___ the
just a - bout time. Does my wed - ding gown ___ look pret - ty, Dad - dy? Dad -

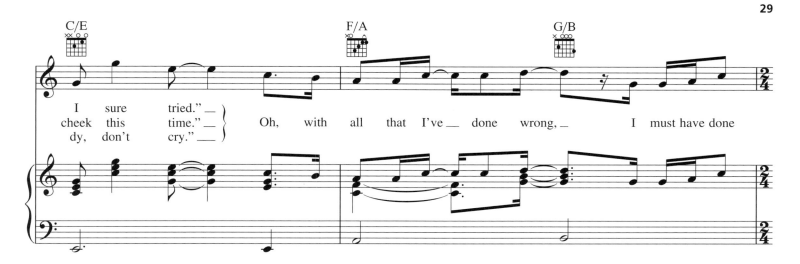

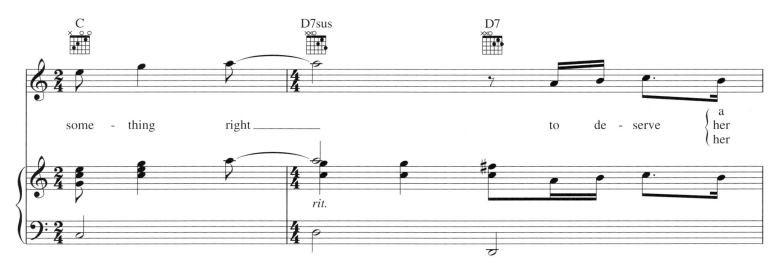

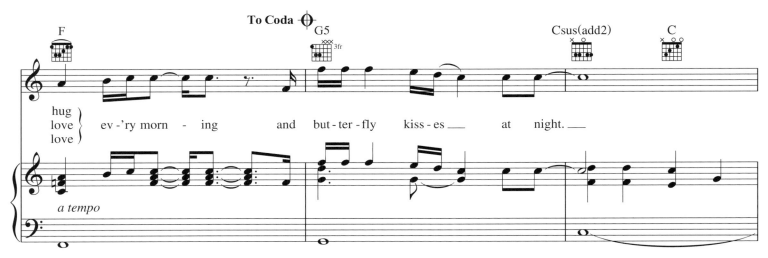

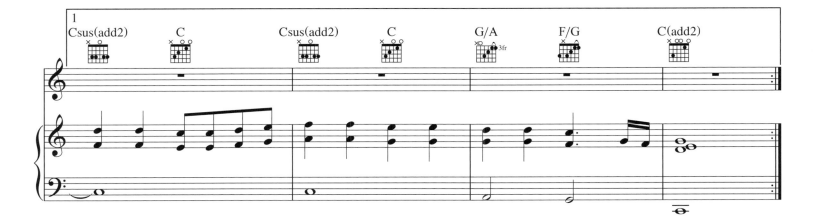

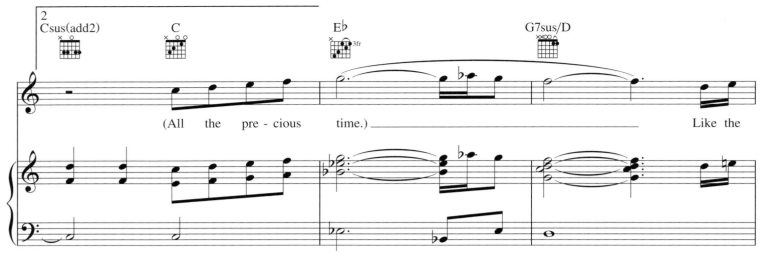

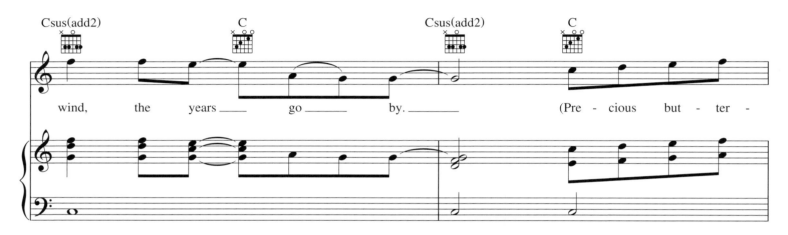

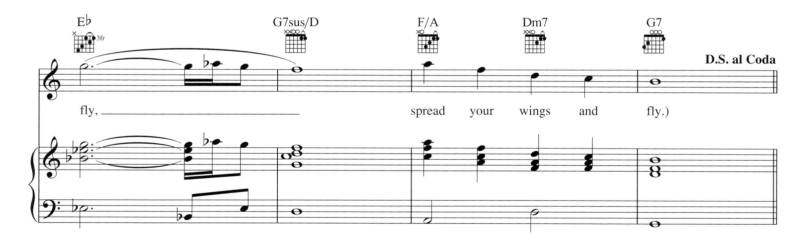

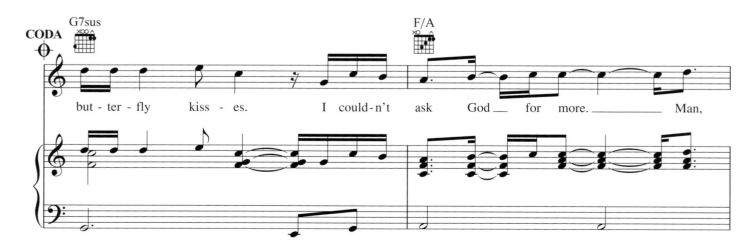

this is what _ love ___ is. _____ I know I've got-ta let _____ her go, but I'll

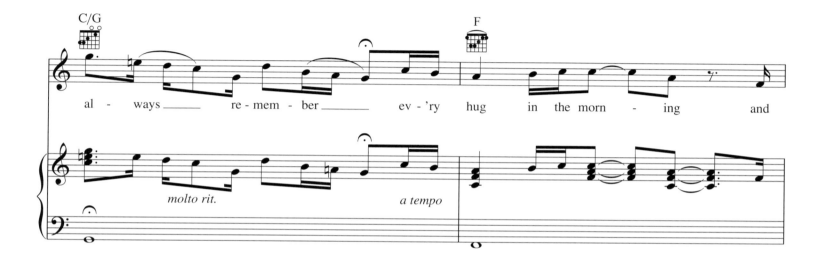

al - ways _____ re-mem-ber _____ ev-'ry hug in the morn - ing _____ and

molto rit.   *a tempo*

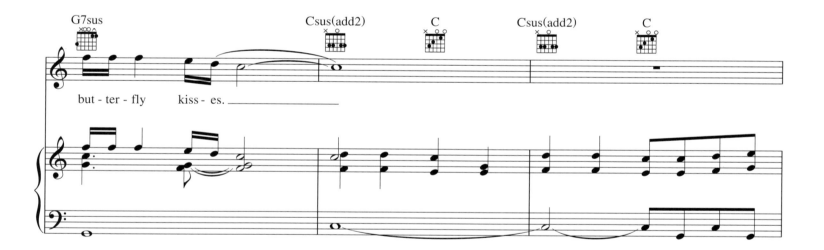

but - ter - fly kiss - es. _____

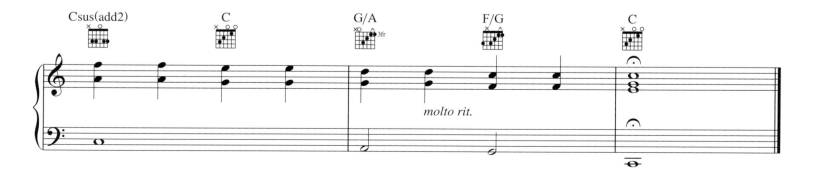

molto rit.

CANDLE ON THE WATER

from Walt Disney's PETE'S DRAGON

Words and Music by AL KASHA
and JOEL HIRSCHHORN

I'll be your can-dle on the wa-ter,
I'll be your can-dle on the wa-ter

my love for you will al-ways
'til ev-'ry wave is warm and

burn.
bright.

I know you're lost
My soul is there

and drift-ing,
be-side you,

but the clouds are lift-ing.
let this can-dle guide you;

Don't give up; you have some-where to turn.
soon you'll see a gold-en stream of

light.

A cold and friend-less tide has found you, don't let the storm-y dark-ness

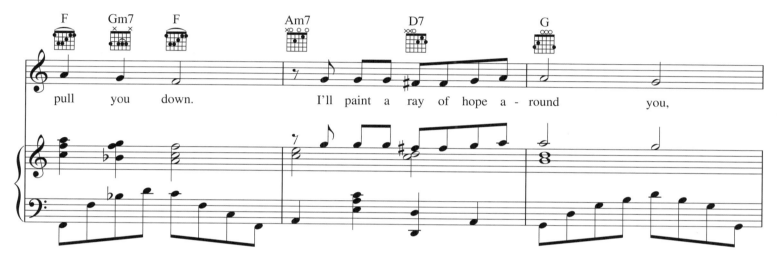

pull you down. I'll paint a ray of hope a-round you,

cir-cling in the air light-ed by a prayer. _____

I'll be your can-dle on the wa-ter, this flame in-side of me will

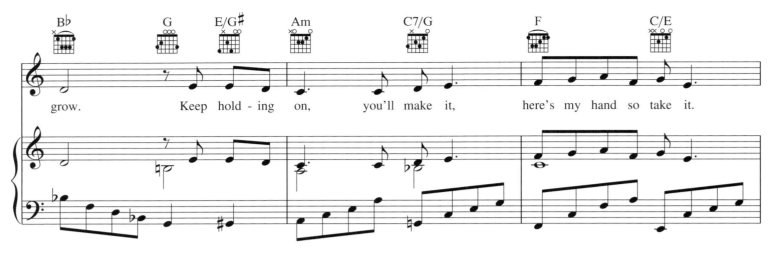

grow. Keep hold - ing on, you'll make it, here's my hand so take it.

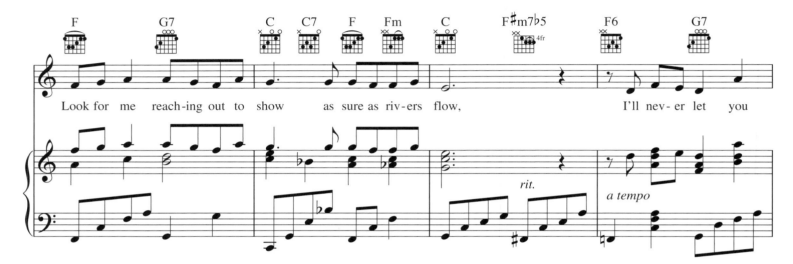

Look for me reach - ing out to show as sure as riv - ers flow, I'll nev - er let you

rit.

a tempo

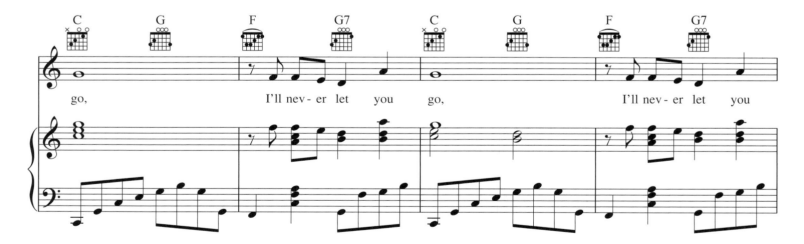

go, I'll nev - er let you go, I'll nev - er let you

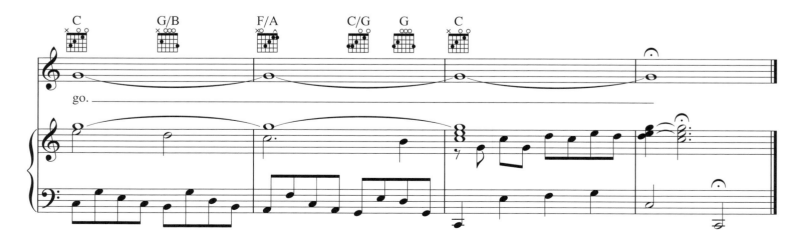

go. _____

FIELDS OF GOLD

Music and Lyrics by
STING

Flowing, moderately

You'll re-mem-ber me, when the west wind moves _ up a -
stay with me, will you be my love _ a -

on the fields _ of bar - ley. You'll for - get the sun in his
mong the fields _ of bar - ley? We'll for - get the sun in his

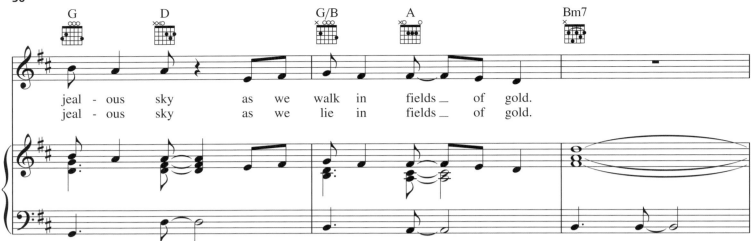

jeal - ous sky   as we walk in   fields __ of gold.
jeal - ous sky   as we lie in   fields __ of gold.

So she
See the

took her love   for to gaze a - while __ up - on the fields __ of bar -
west wind move   like a lov - er so __ up - on the fields __ of bar -

- ley.   In his arms she fell   as her hair came down   a - mong __
- ley.   Feel her bod - y rise   when you kiss her mouth   a - mong __

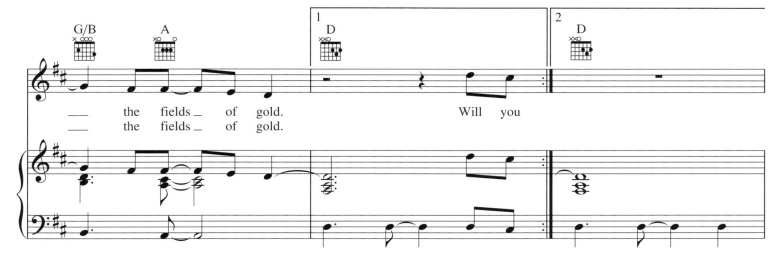

the fields __ of gold. Will you
the fields __ of gold.

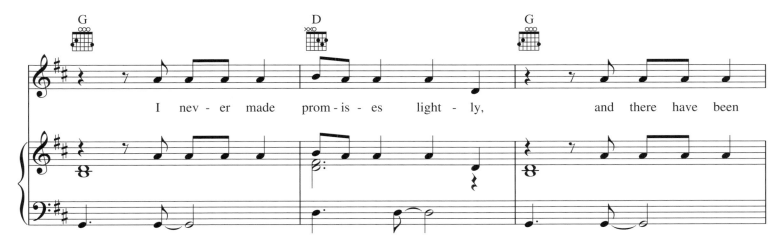

I nev-er made prom-is-es light-ly, and there have been

some that I've bro-ken, but I swear __ in the days still left we'll walk __

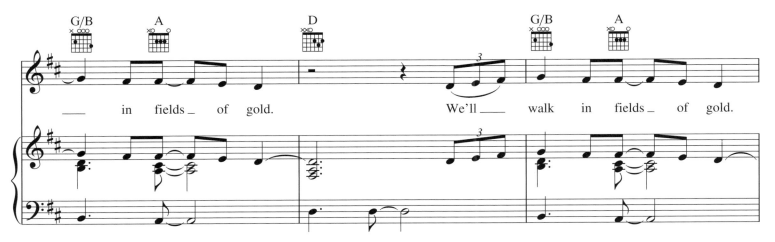

__ in fields __ of gold. We'll __ walk in fields __ of gold.

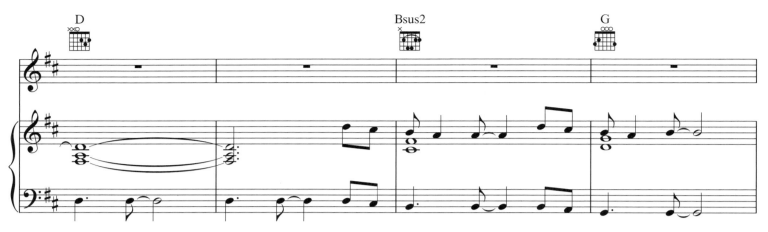

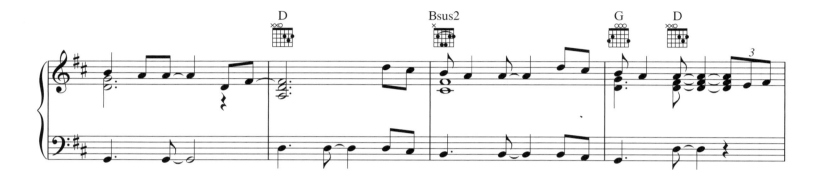

Man - y years have passed since those _

mem - ber me when the _

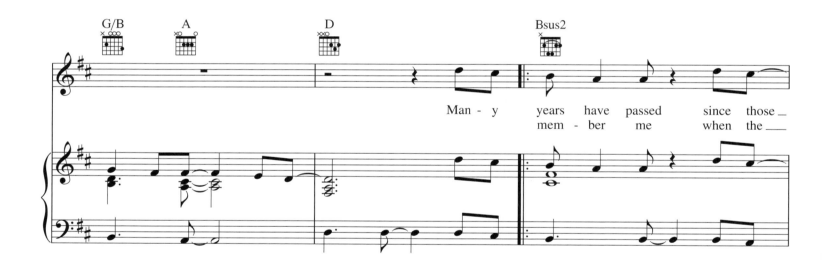

_ sum - mer days a - mong the fields _ of bar - ley. See the

_ west wind moves up - on the fields _ of bar - ley. You can

chil - dren run as the sun goes down a - mong ___ the fields ___ of gold.
tell the sun in his jeal - ous sky when we walked in fields ___ of gold,

You'll re - when ___ we walked in fields ___ of gold,

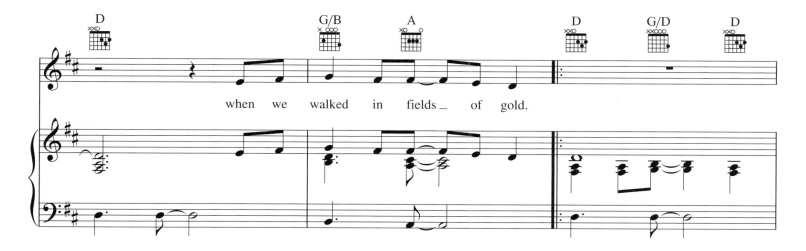

when we walked in fields ___ of gold.

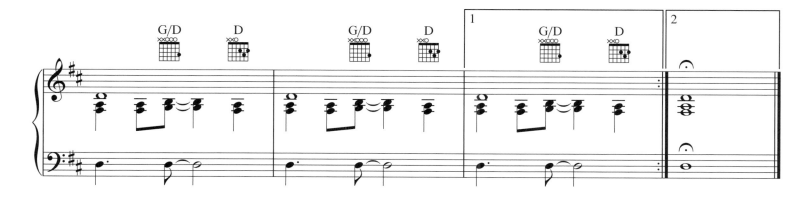

CHANGE THE WORLD

Words and Music by WAYNE KIRKPATRICK,
GORDON KENNEDY and TOMMY SIMS

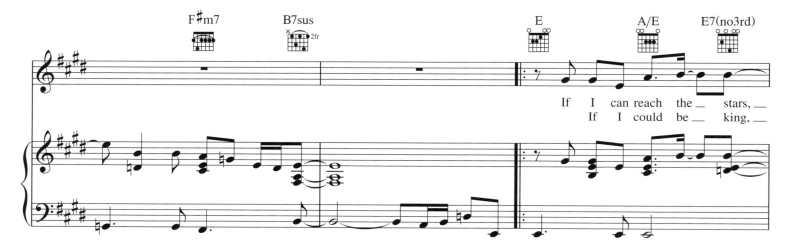

If I can reach the __ stars, __
If I could be __ king, __

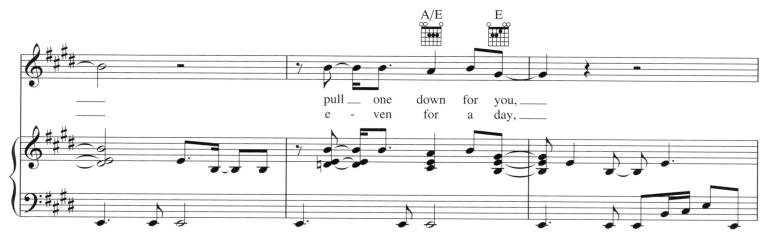

pull __ one down for you, __
e - ven for a day, __

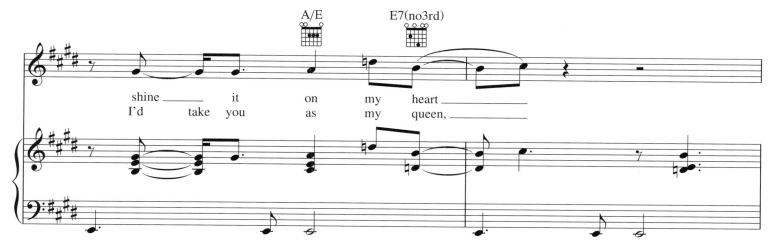

shine _____ it on my heart _____
I'd take you as my queen, _____

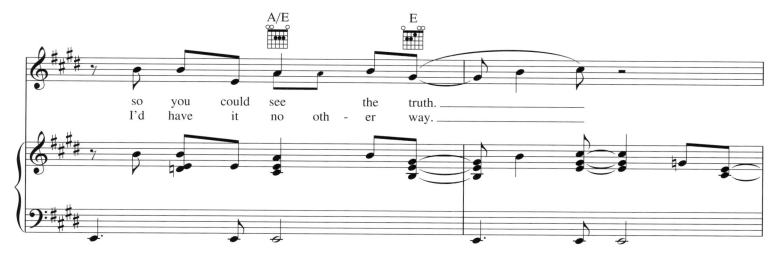

so you could see the truth. _____
I'd have it no oth - er way. _____

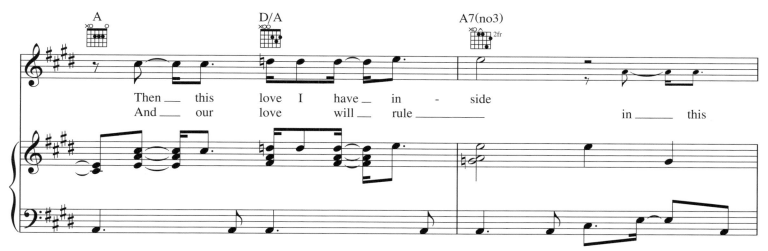

Then ___ this love I have ___ in - side
And ___ our love will ___ rule _____ in ___ this

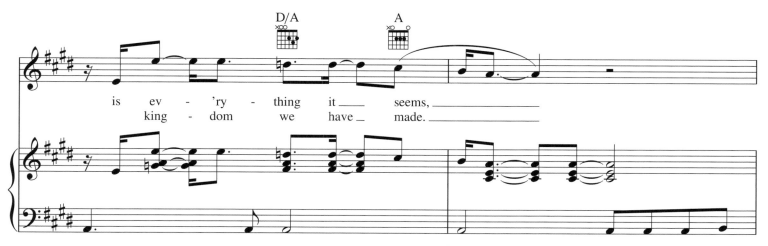

is ev - 'ry - thing it _____ seems, _____
king - dom we have ___ made. _____

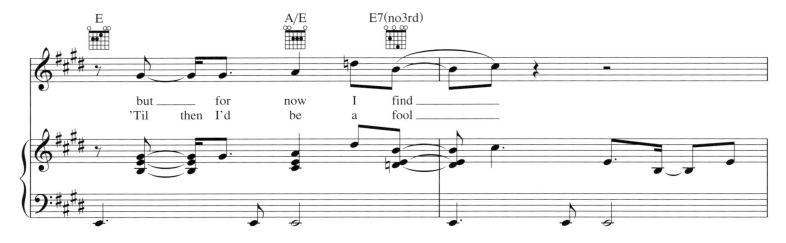

but _____ for now I find _____
'Til then I'd be a fool _____

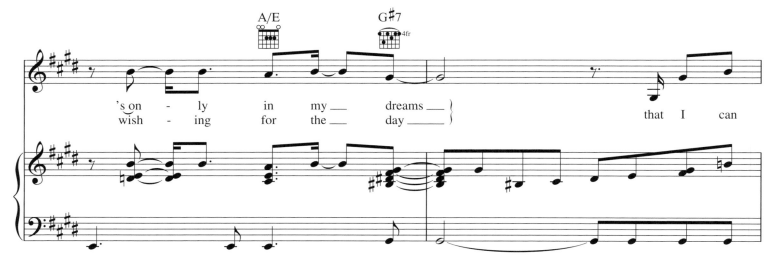

's on - ly in my ___ dreams ___ }
wish - ing for the ___ day _____ }
that I can

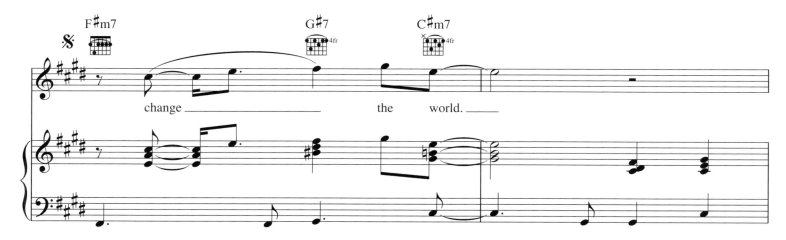

change _____ the world. _____

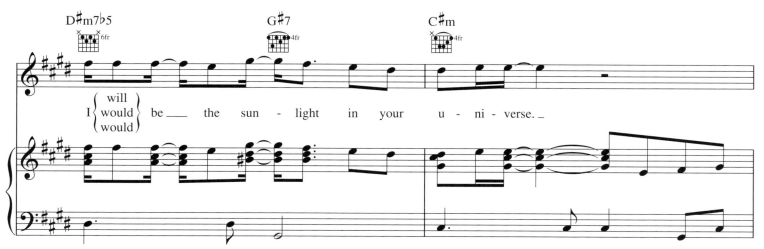

I { will / would / would } be ___ the sun - light in your u - ni - verse. _

You would think ___ my love ___ was real - ly some - thing ___ good, ba - by, ___

To Coda ⊕

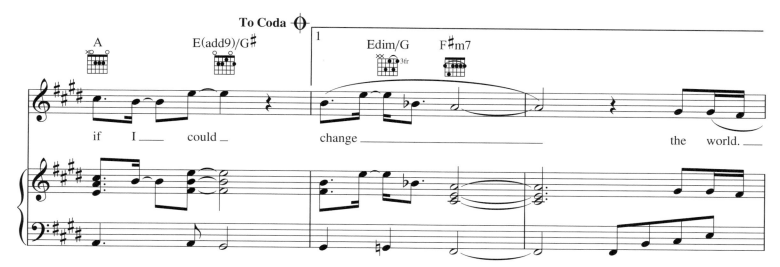

if I ___ could ___ change _____ the world. ___

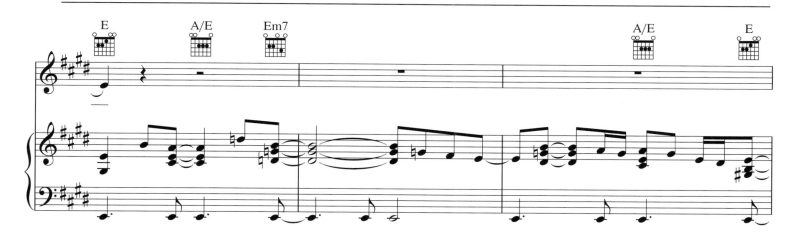

change _____ the world, ___

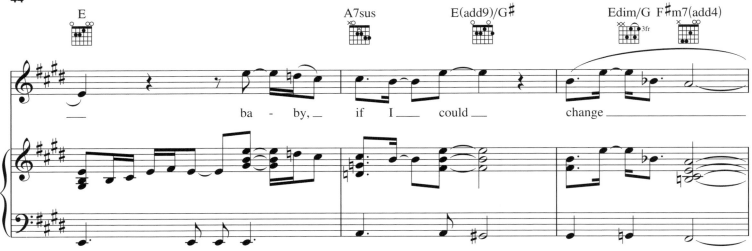

ba - by, if I could change the world.

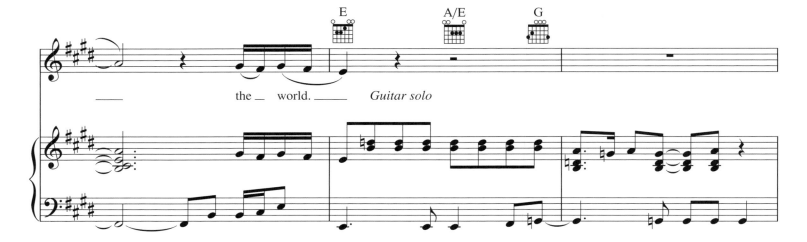

the world. *Guitar solo*

D.S. al Coda

Solo ends I could

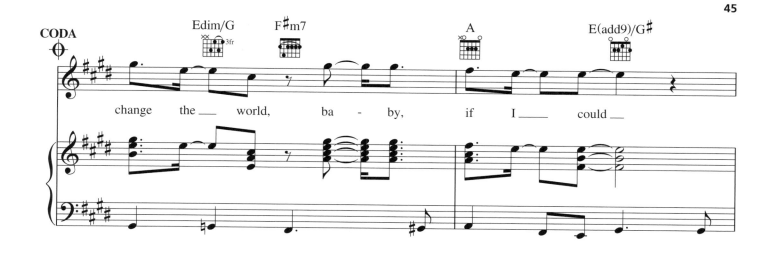

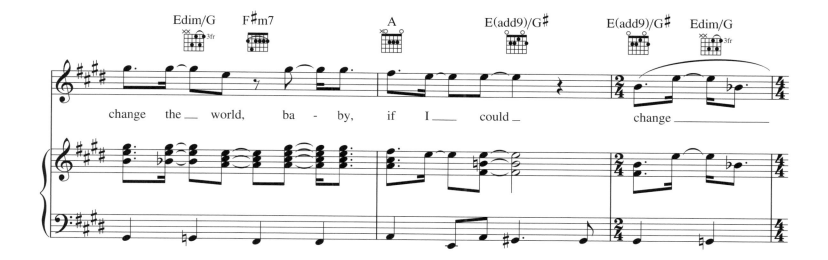

FOREVER YOUNG

Words and Music by ROD STEWART, JIM CREGAN,
KEVIN SAVIGAR and BOB DYLAN

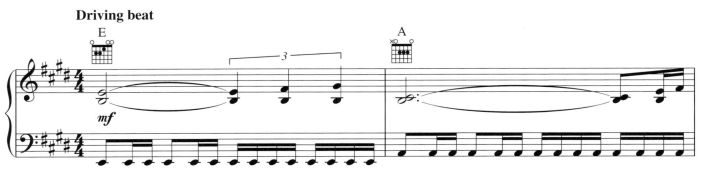

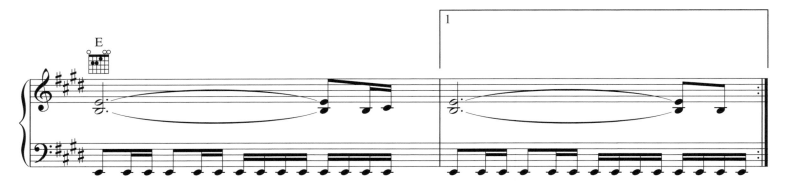

May the good Lord be with you down ev-er-y road you roam.

And may sun-shine and hap-pi-ness sur-

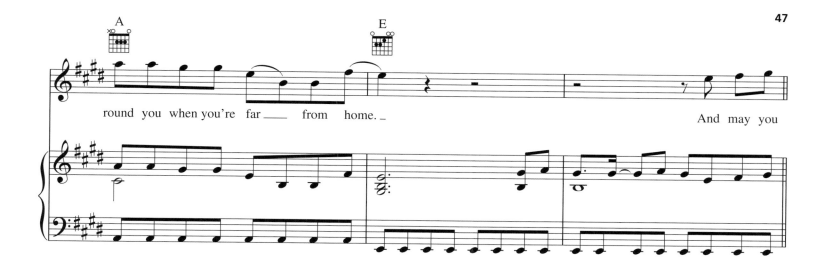

round you when you're far___ from home. ___ And may you

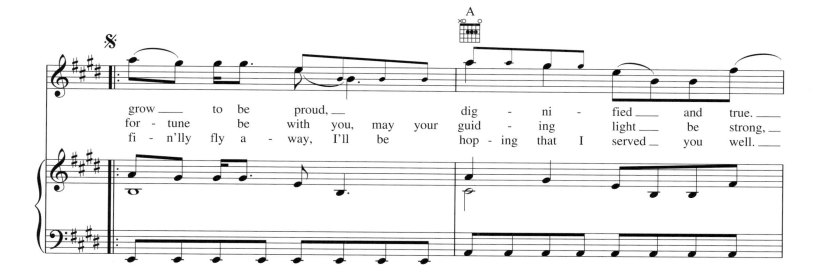

grow ___ to be proud, ___ dig - ni - fied ___ and true. ___
for - tune be with you, may your guid - ing light ___ be strong, ___
fi - n'lly fly a - way, I'll be hop - ing that I served ___ you well. ___

— And do un - to oth - ers as
build a stair-way to heav - en with a
For all the wis-dom of a life - time,

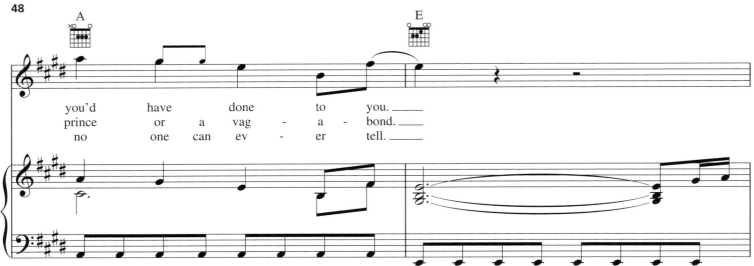

you'd have done to you. _____
prince or a vag - a - bond. _____
no one can ev - er tell. _____

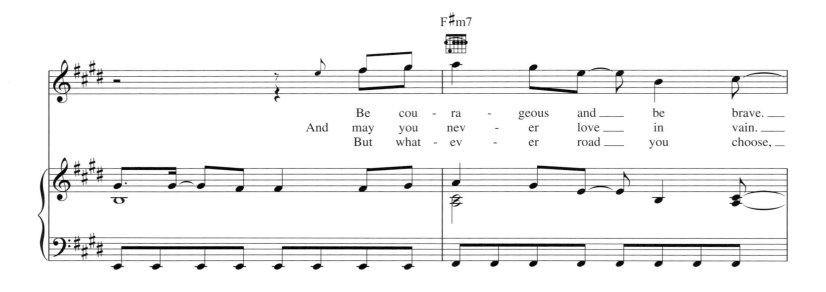

Be cou - ra - geous and _____ be brave. ___
And may you nev - er love _____ in vain. _____
But what - ev - er road _____ you choose, _

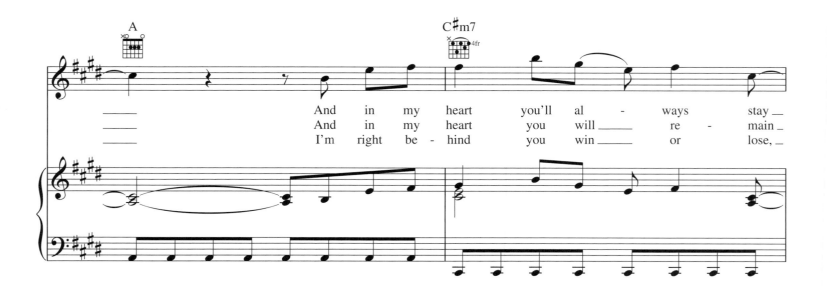

_____ And in my heart you'll al - ways stay _
_____ And in my heart you will _____ re - main _
_____ I'm right be - hind you win _____ or lose, _

for - ev - er young. (For - ev - er

young) For - ev - er young. (For - ev - er

1

young) _____ May good

2, 3

young) _____

F#m7

For

A

\- ev - er

young. _____

For - ev - er _____

To Coda ⊕

young. _

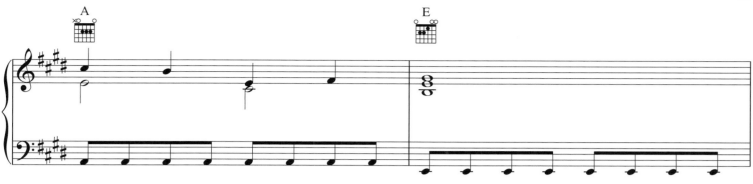

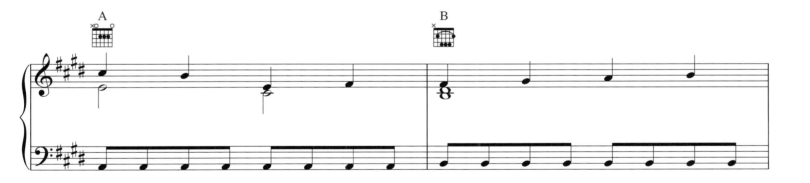

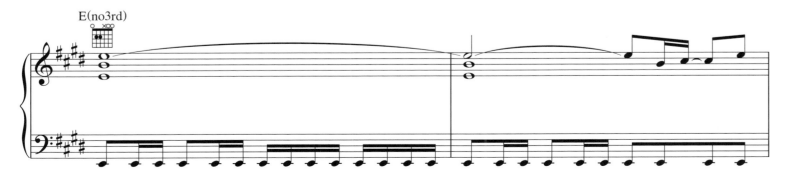

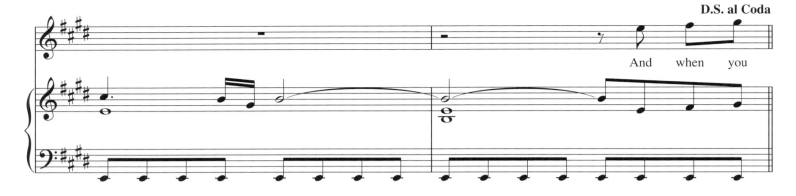

D.S. al Coda

And when you

CODA

F#m7

A

For

For - ev - er

E

young.

F#m7

A

E

For - ev - er young.

FROM A DISTANCE

Words and Music by
JULIE GOLD

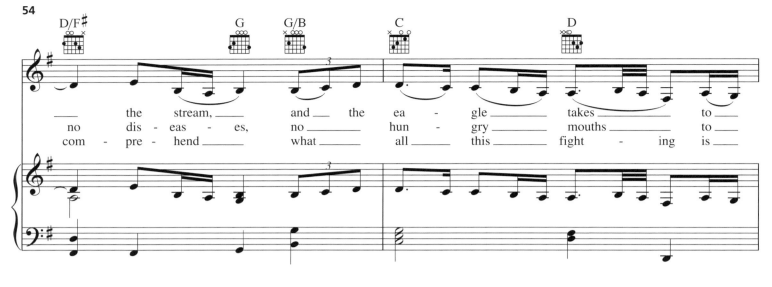

the stream, _____ and ___ the ea - gle _____ takes _____ to ___
no dis - eas - es, no _____ hun - gry _____ mouths _____ to ___
com - pre - hend _____ what _____ all _____ this _____ fight - ing is ___

flight. From ___ a dis - tance there ___ is _____ har -
feed. From ___ a dis - tance, we _____ are
for. From ___ a dis - tance, there ___ is _____ har -

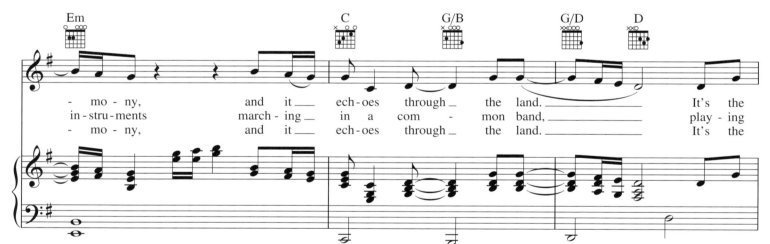

- mo - ny, and it ___ ech - oes through ___ the land. _____ It's the
in - stru - ments march - ing ___ in a com - mon band, _____ play - ing
- mo - ny, and it ___ ech - oes through ___ the land. _____ It's the

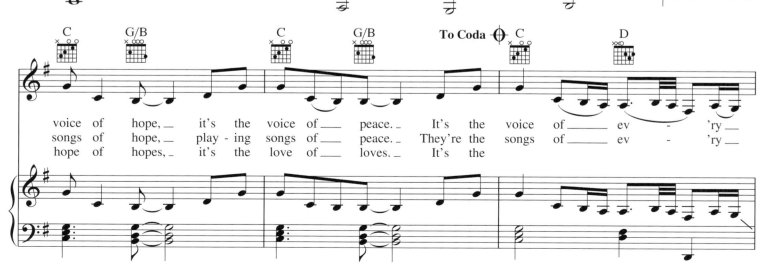

voice of hope, ___ it's the voice of ___ peace. It's the voice of _____ ev - 'ry ___
songs of hope, ___ play - ing songs of ___ peace. They're the songs of _____ ev - 'ry ___
hope of hopes, ___ it's the love of ___ loves. It's the

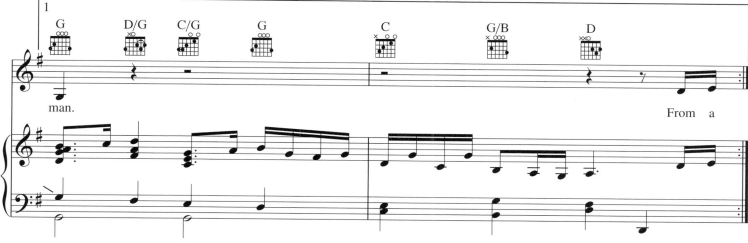

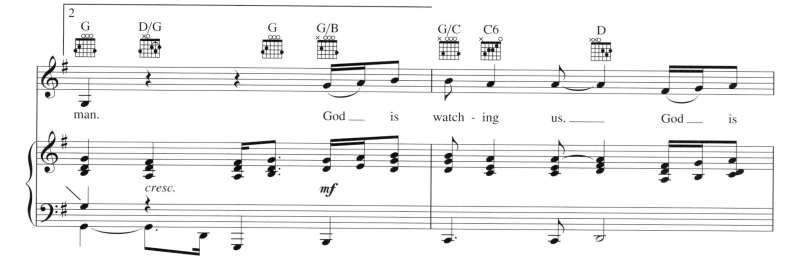

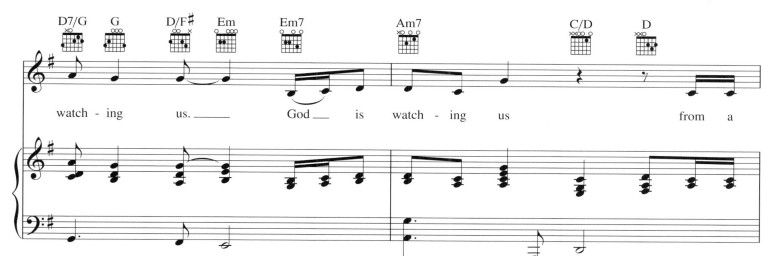

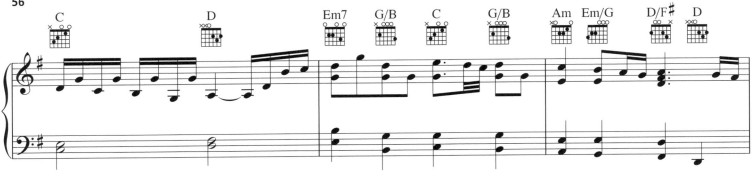

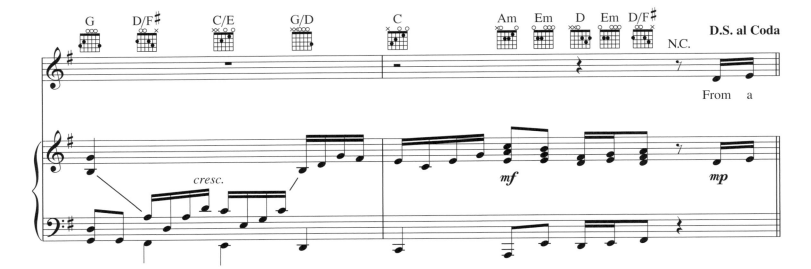

From a

heart _____ of ev - 'ry ___ man. _____ It's the

hope of ___ hopes, ___ it's the love of ___ loves. ___ This is the song ___ of _____ ev - 'ry

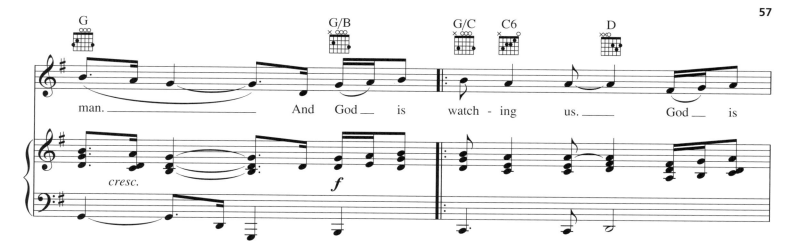

man._____ And God __ is watch - ing us._____ God __ is

watch - ing us._____ God __ is watch - ing us from a _____

dis - tance._____ Oh, God is ____ watch - ing us _____ from a

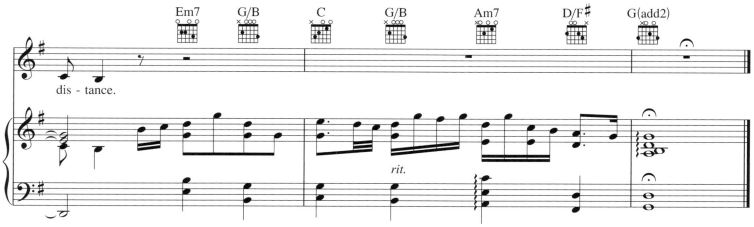

dis - tance.

FRIENDS

Words and Music by MICHAEL W. SMITH
and DEBORAH D. SMITH

Moderately slow

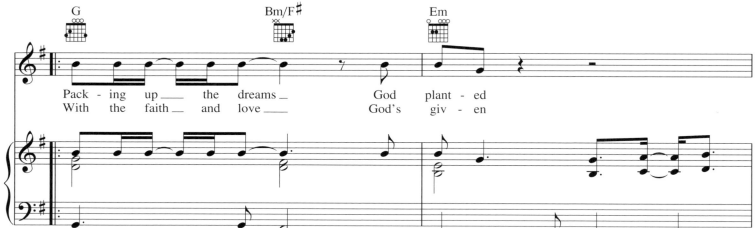

Pack - ing up ___ the dreams ___ God plant - ed
With the faith ___ and love ___ God's giv - en

in the fer - tile soil ___ of ___ you,
spring - ing from __ the hope ___ we __ know,

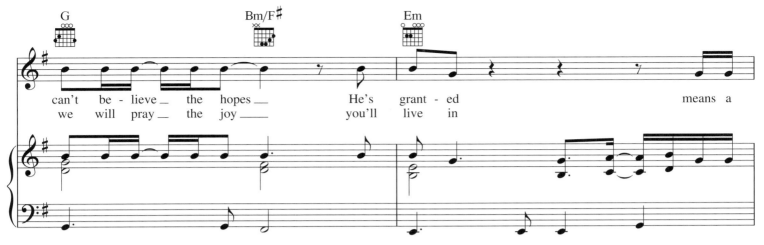

can't be-lieve _ the hopes _ He's grant-ed means a
we will pray _ the joy _____ you'll live in

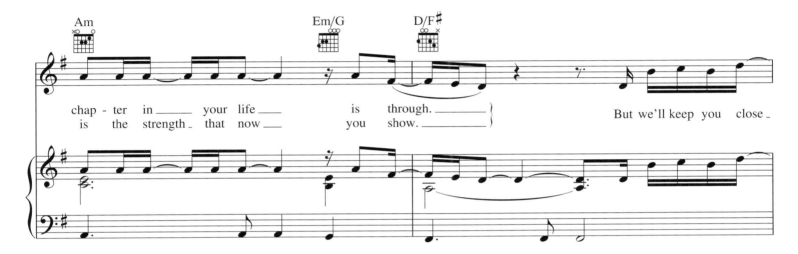

chap-ter in _____ your life _____ is through. _____ But we'll keep you close _
is the strength _ that now _ you show. _____

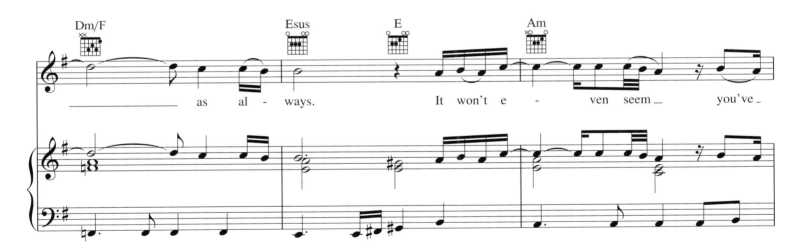

_____ as al-ways. It won't e-ven seem _ you've _

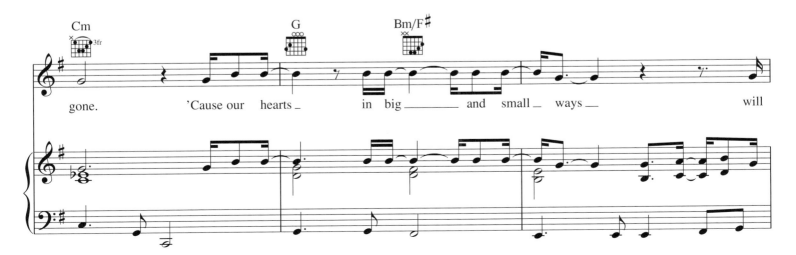

gone. 'Cause our hearts _ in big _____ and small _ ways _____ will

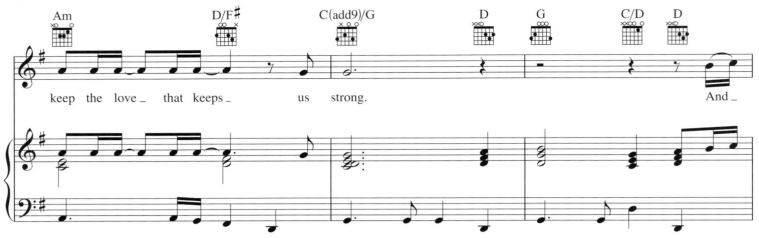

keep the love _ that keeps _ us strong. And _

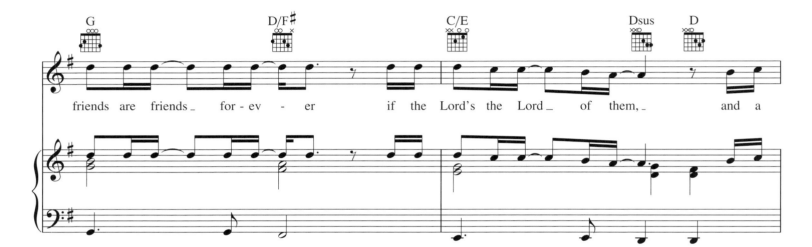

friends are friends _ for - ev - er if the Lord's the Lord _ of them, _ and a

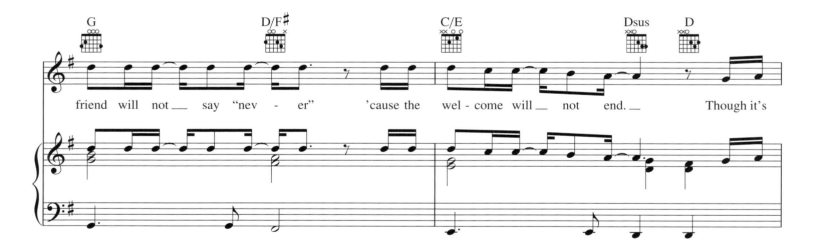

friend will not _ say "nev - er" 'cause the wel - come will _ not end. _ Though it's

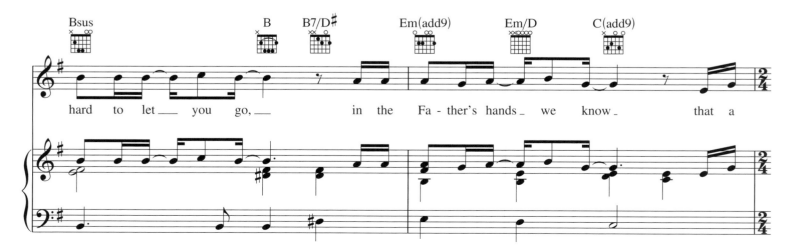

hard to let _ you go, _ in the Fa - ther's hands _ we know _ that a

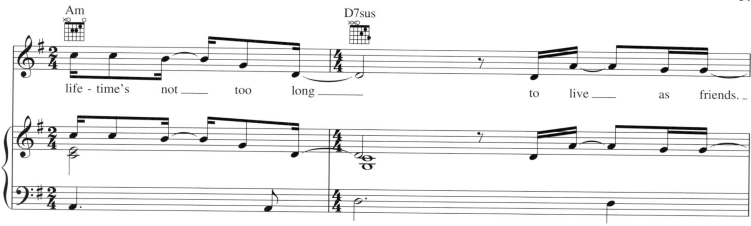

life - time's not ___ too long _____ to live ___ as friends. _

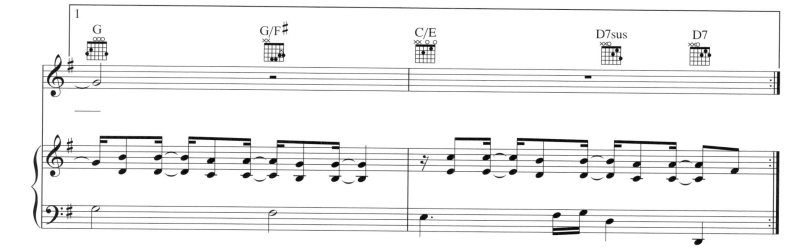

___ And ___ friends are friends _ for - ev - er if the

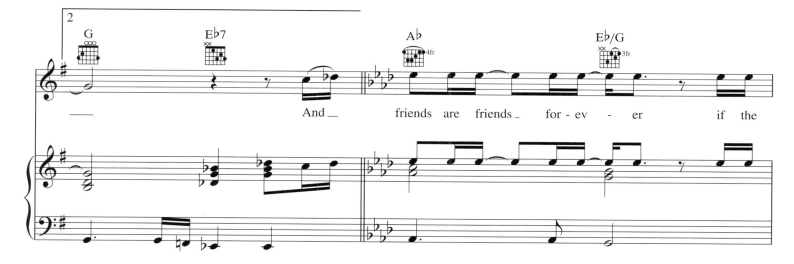

Lord's the Lord _ of them, _ and a friend will not ___ say "nev - er" 'cause the

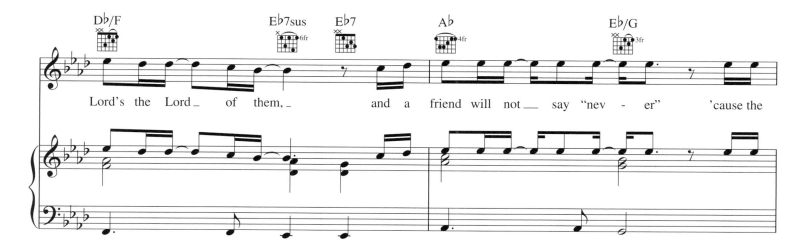

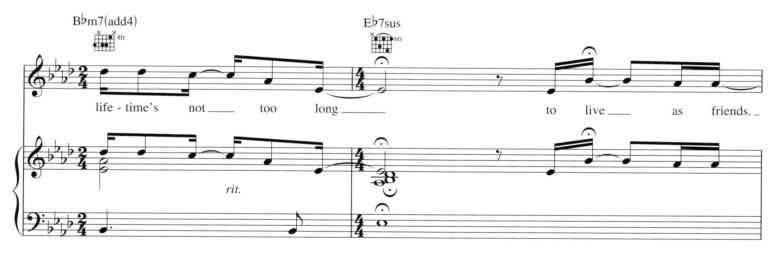

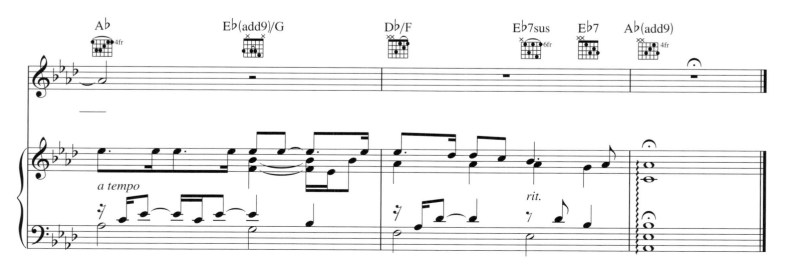

HAPPY TOGETHER

Words and Music by GARRY BONNER
and ALAN GORDON

I can see me lov- in' no- bod - y but you for all my life. __

__ When you're with me, ba - by, the skies -'ll be

blue for all my life. ____ Me and you, ____ and you and

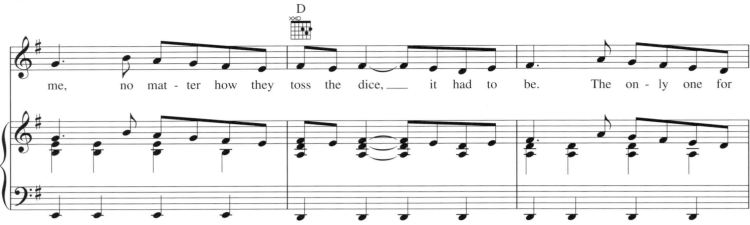

me, no mat - ter how they toss the dice, ___ it had to be. The on - ly one for

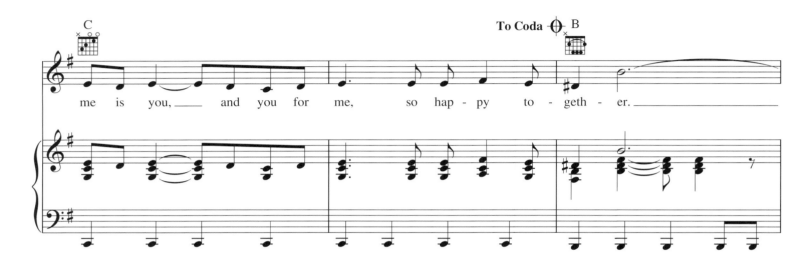

me is you, ___ and you for me, so hap - py to - geth - er. ___

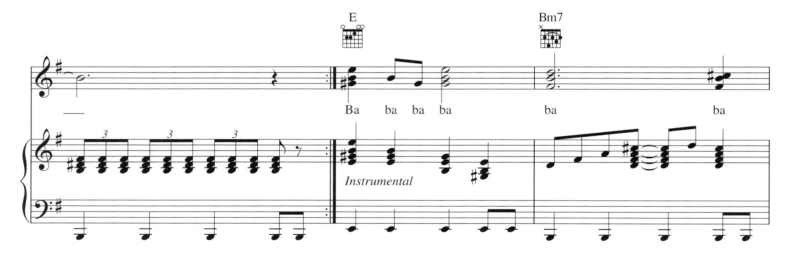

Ba ba ba ba ba ba

Instrumental

ba ba ba ba ba. ___ Ba ba ba ba

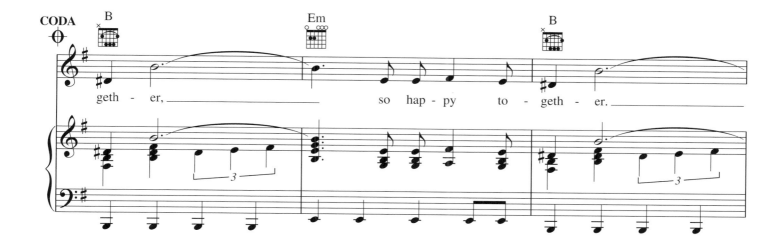

I BELIEVE IN YOU AND ME

from the Touchstone Motion Picture THE PREACHER'S WIFE

Words and Music by DAVID WOLFERT
and SANDY LINZER

Slow Ballad

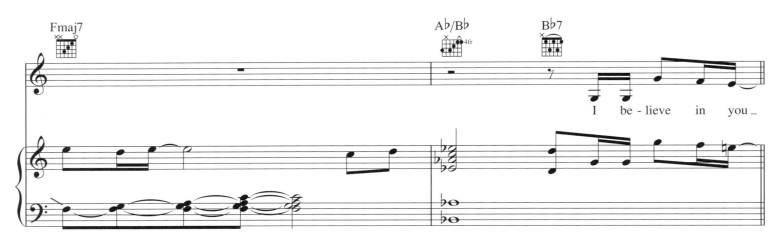

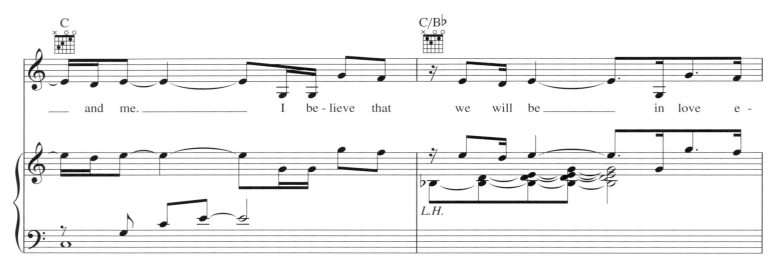

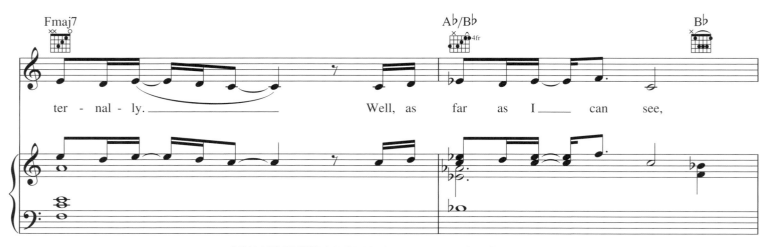

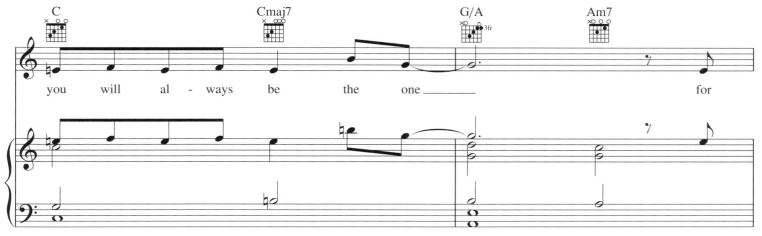

you will al - ways be the one _____ for

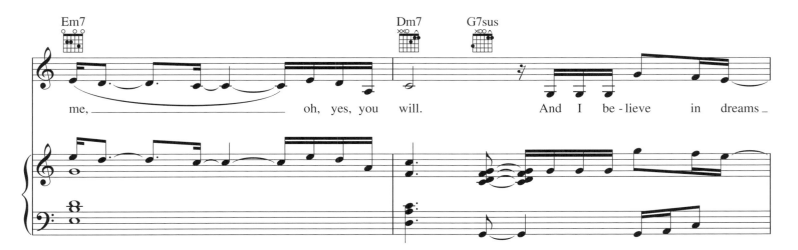

me, _____ oh, yes, you will. And I be - lieve in dreams _

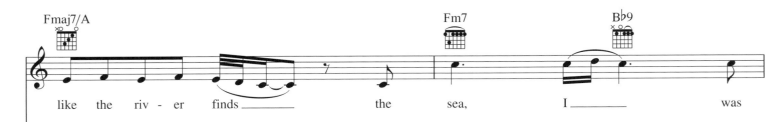

_____ a - gain. _____ I be - lieve that love will nev - er end. _____ And

like the riv - er finds _____ the sea, I _____ was

lost, _____ now I'm ___ free _____ 'cause

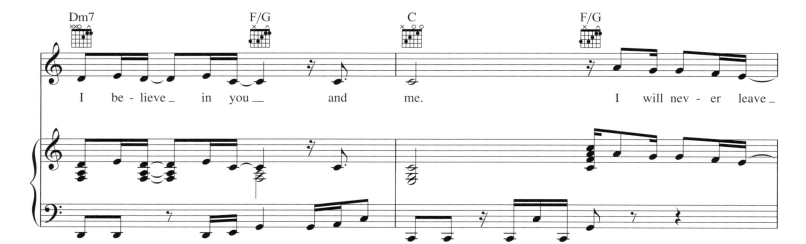

I be - lieve ___ in you ___ and me. I will nev - er leave ___

___ your side. ___ I will nev - er hurt ___ your ___ pride. _____ When all the

chips are down, ___ babe, then I will al-ways be ___ a - round. ___

Just to be right where you are, _____ my

love. _____ You know I love _ you, boy. ___ I'll nev-er

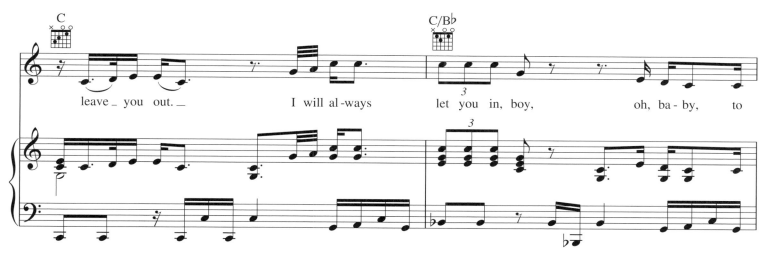

leave _ you out. __ I will al-ways let you in, boy, oh, ba-by, to

plac-es no one's ev - er been. ___ Deep _____ in-side, ____

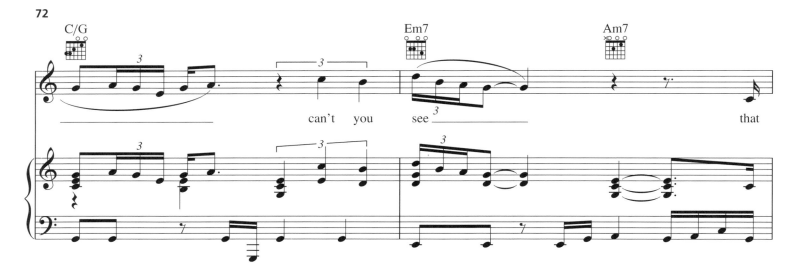

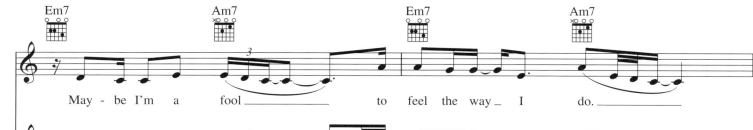

me. See, I'm __ lost, _____ now I'm

free _____ 'cause I be-lieve in you and _____

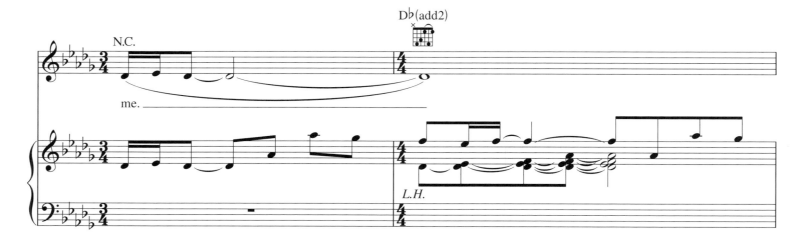

me. _____

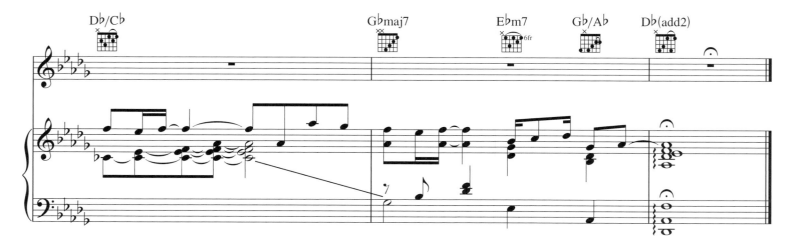

I BELIEVE MY HEART

from THE WOMAN IN WHITE

Music by ANDREW LLOYD WEBBER
Lyrics by DAVID ZIPPEL

Moderately

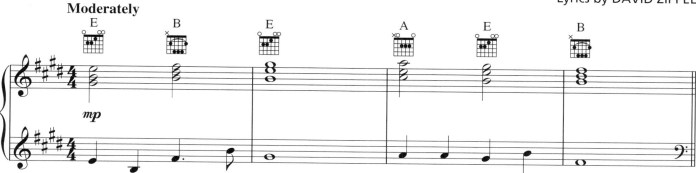

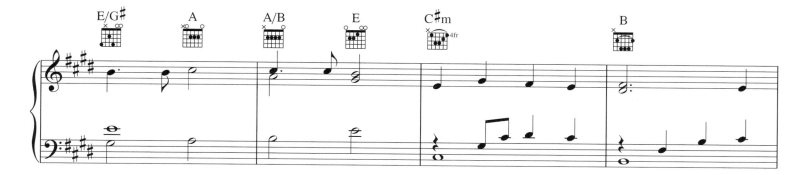

HARTRIGHT:

When-ev - er I look at you, ___ the world dis - ap -

pears. All in a sin - gle glance so re - veal - ing. ___

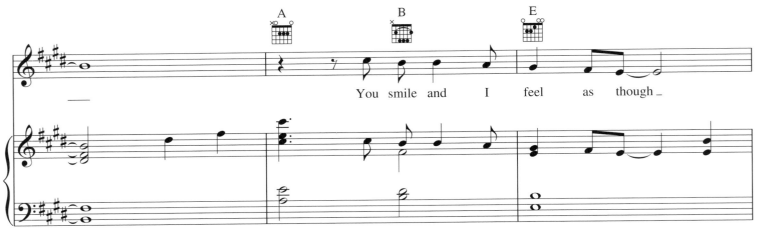

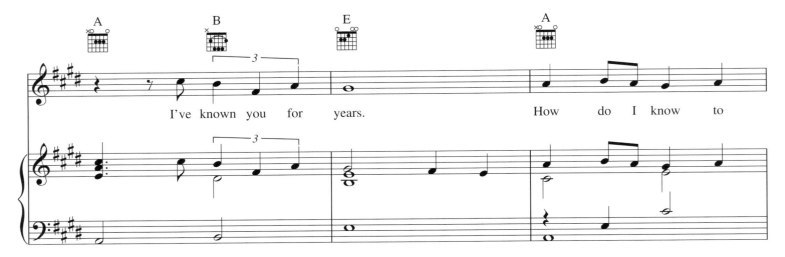

You smile and I feel as though __
I've known you for years. How do I know to

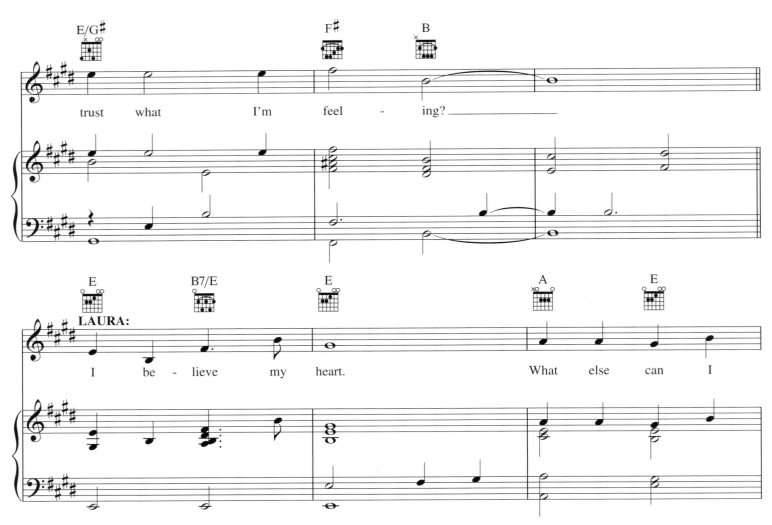

trust what I'm feel - ing? _____
LAURA: I be - lieve my heart. What else can I

do when ev - 'ry part of ev - 'ry thought

leads me straight to you? **HARTRIGHT:** I be - lieve my heart.

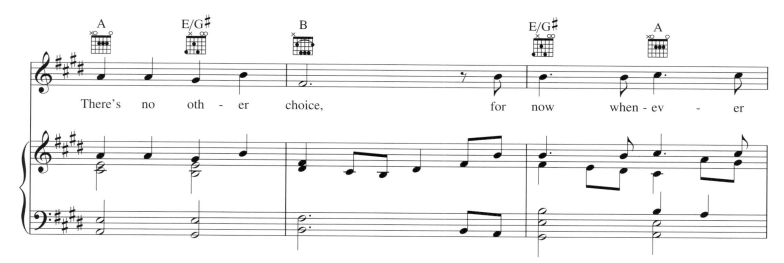

There's no oth - er choice, for now when - ev - er

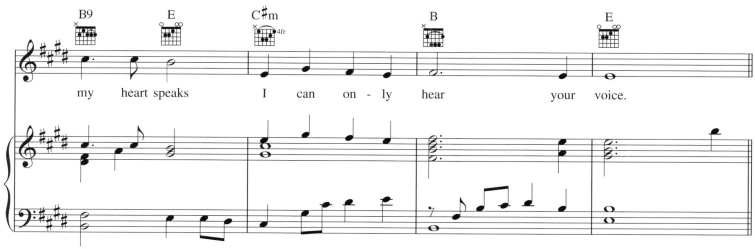

my heart speaks I can on - ly hear your voice.

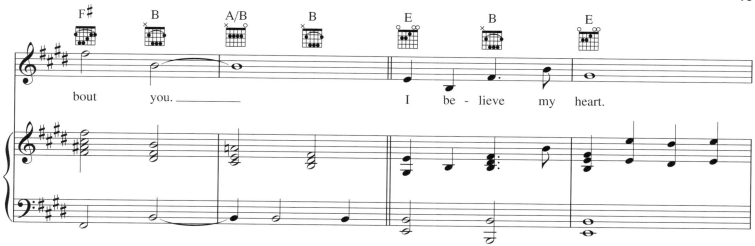

bout you. _____ I be - lieve my heart.

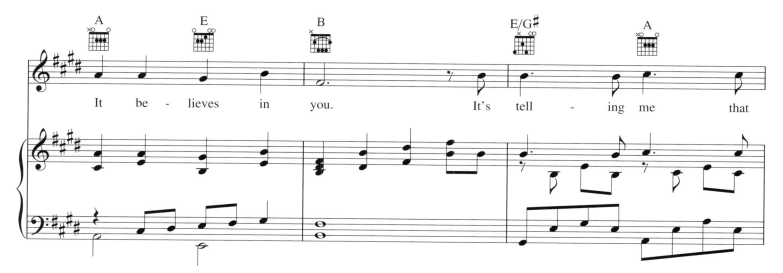

It be - lieves in you. It's tell - ing me that

what I see is com - plete - ly true.

LAURA:

I be - lieve my heart. How can it be

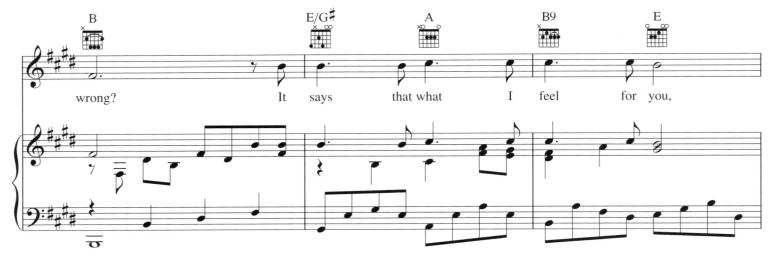

wrong? It says that what I feel for you,

I will feel my whole life long.

BOTH:

I be - lieve my heart. It be - lieves in

you. It's tell - ing me that what I see

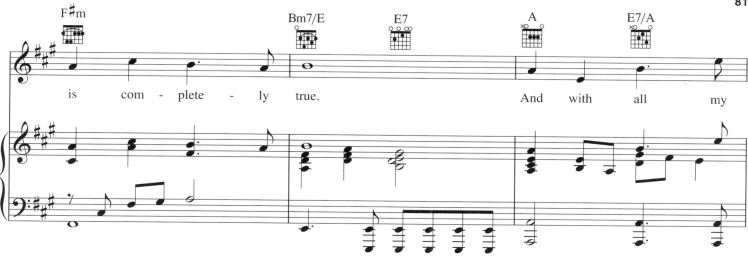

is com-plete-ly true. And with all my

soul I be - lieve my heart. The

por - trait that it paints of you is a per - fect

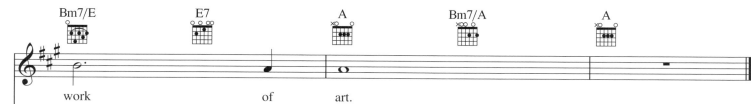

work of art.

I HOPE YOU DANCE

Words and Music by TIA SILLERS
and MARK D. SANDERS

Moderately

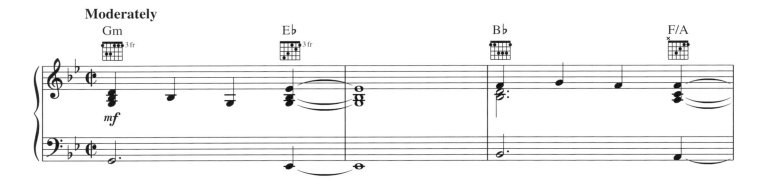

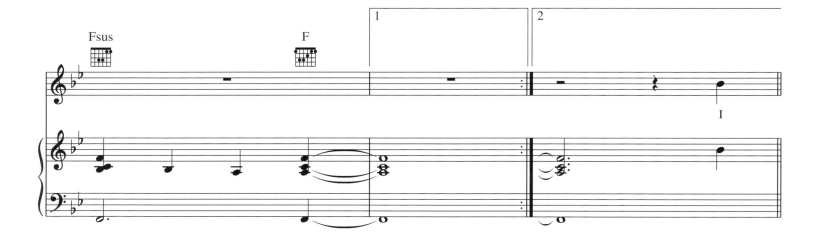

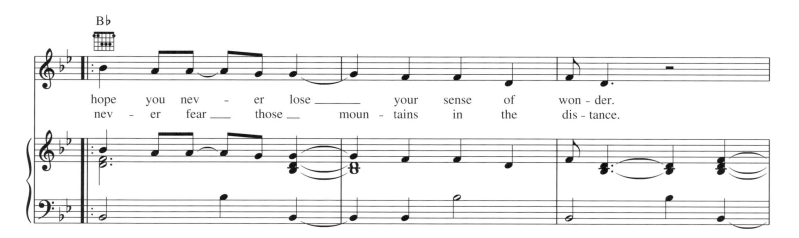

hope you nev - er lose _____ your sense of won - der.
nev - er fear _____ those _____ moun - tains in the dis - tance.

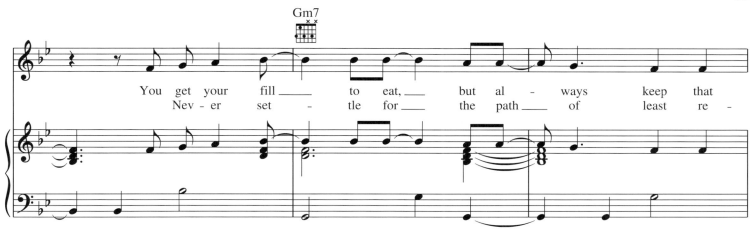

You get your fill ___ to eat, ___ but al - ways keep that
Nev - er set - tle for ___ the path ___ of least re -

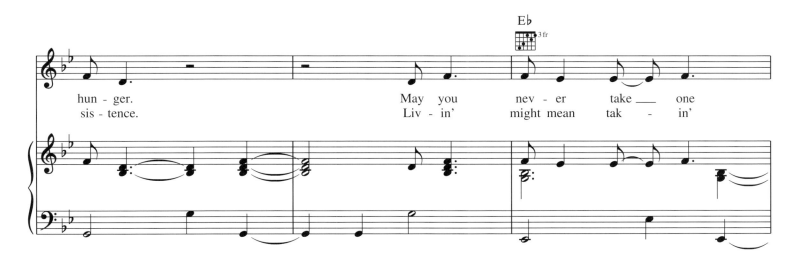

hun - ger. May you nev - er take ___ one
sis - tence. Liv - in' might mean tak - in'

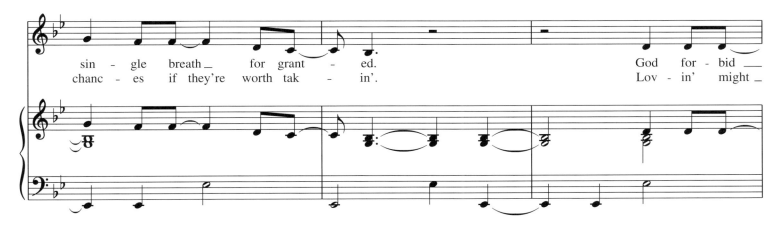

sin - gle breath ___ for grant - ed. God for - bid ___
chanc - es if they're worth tak - in'. Lov - in' might ___

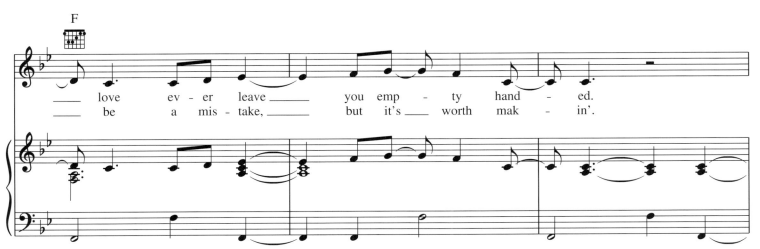

___ love ev - er leave ___ you emp - ty hand - ed.
___ be a mis - take, ___ but it's ___ worth mak - in'.

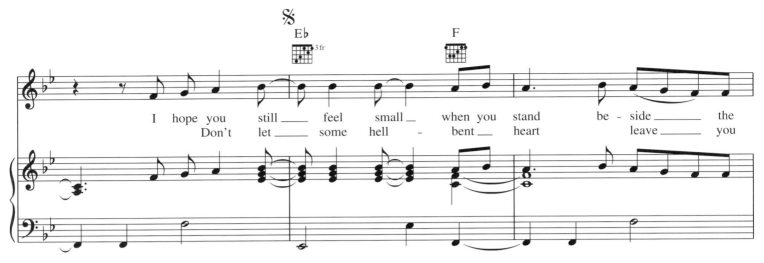

I hope you still __ feel small __ when you stand __ be-side __ the
Don't let __ some hell - bent __ heart leave __ you

o - cean.
bit - ter.
When-ev - er one __ door clos - es, I __
When you come close __ to sell - in' out, __

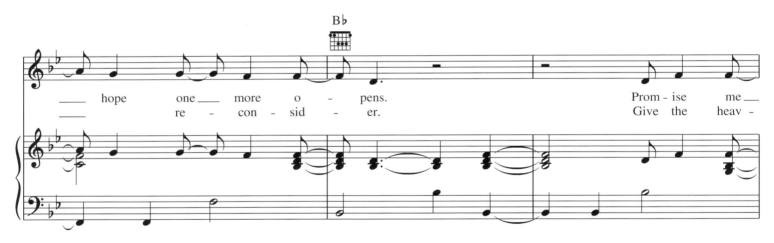

__ hope one __ more o - pens.
__ re - con - sid - er.
Prom - ise me __
Give the heav -

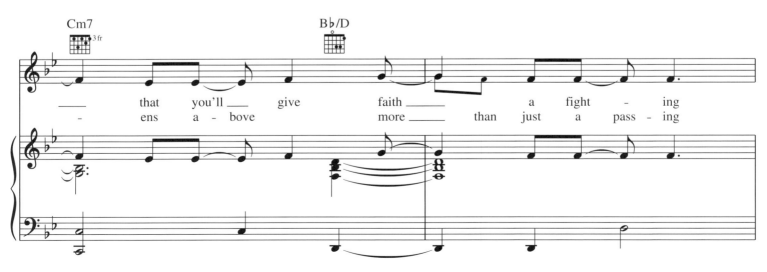

__ that you'll __ give faith __ a fight - ing
- ens a - bove more __ than just a pass - ing

chance.
glance. And when you get the choice to

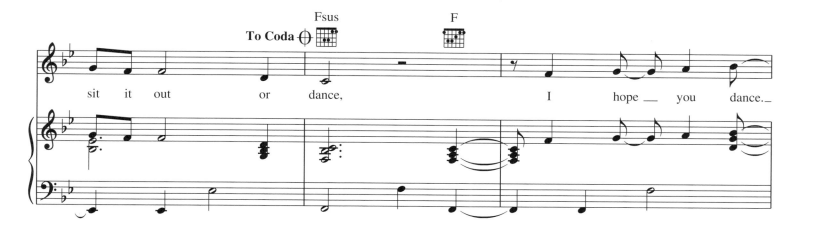

sit it out or dance, I hope you dance.

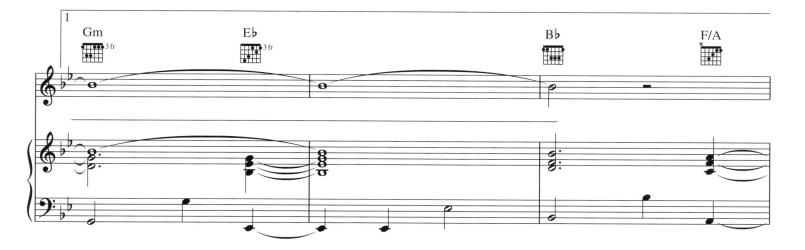

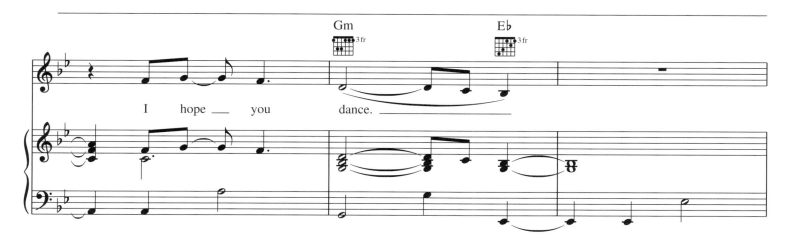

I hope you dance.

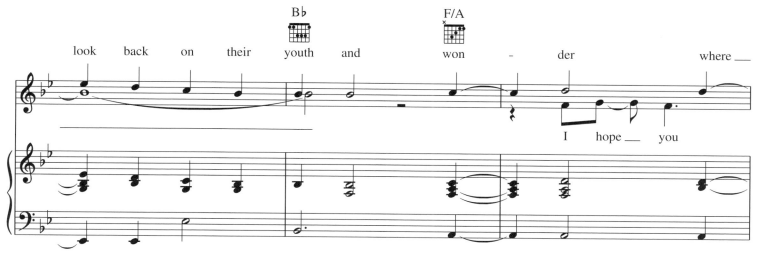

look back on their youth and won - der where ___

I hope ___ you

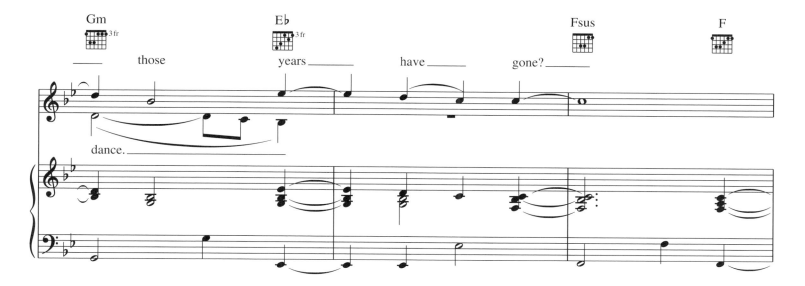

___ those years ___ have ___ gone? ___

dance. ___

D.S. al Coda

I hope ___ you still ___

CODA

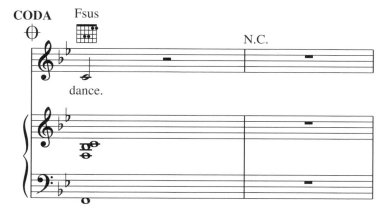

dance.

N.C.

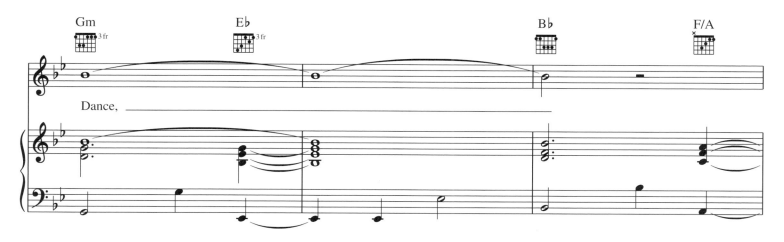

Dance, ___

IMAGINE

Words and Music by
JOHN LENNON

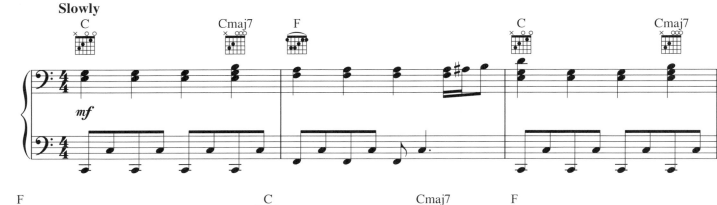

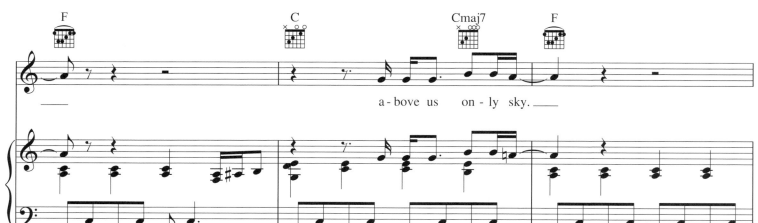

Lyrics: I-mag-ine there's no heav-en. It's eas-y if you try. No hell be-low us, a-bove us on-ly sky.

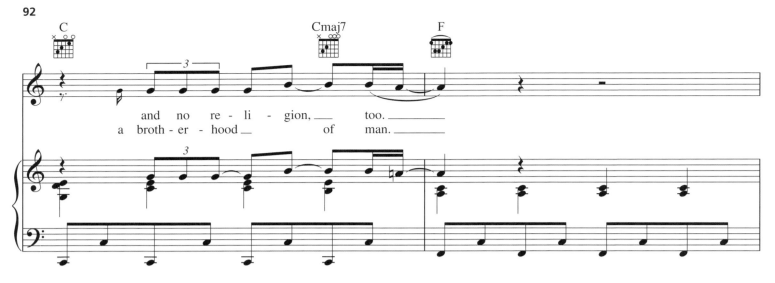

and no re - li - gion, ___ too. ___
a broth - er - hood ___ of man. ___

I - mag - ine all the peo - ple ___
I - mag - ine all the peo - ple ___

liv - ing life in peace. ___
shar - ing all the world. ___

You, _____ you may say ___ I'm a

dream - er,

but I'm not the on - ly one. ___

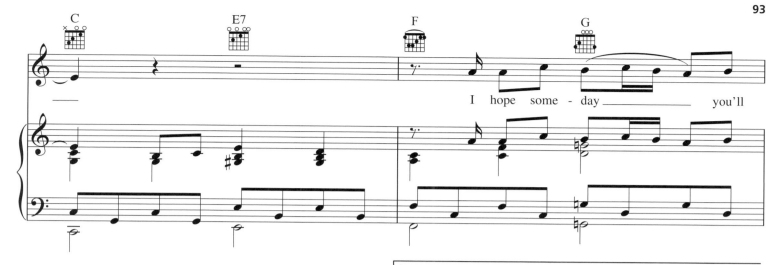

I hope some - day _____ you'll

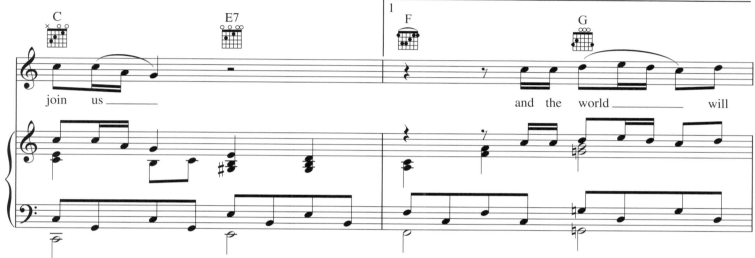

join us _____ and the world _____ will

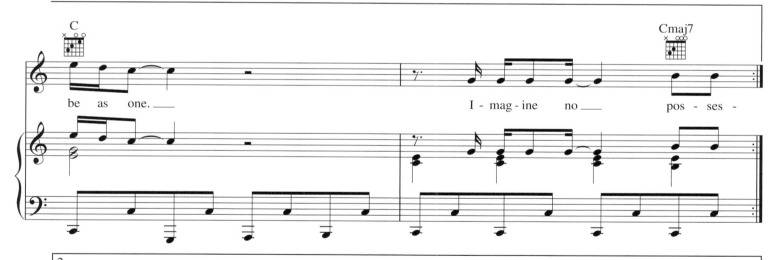

be as one. ___ I - mag - ine no ___ pos - ses -

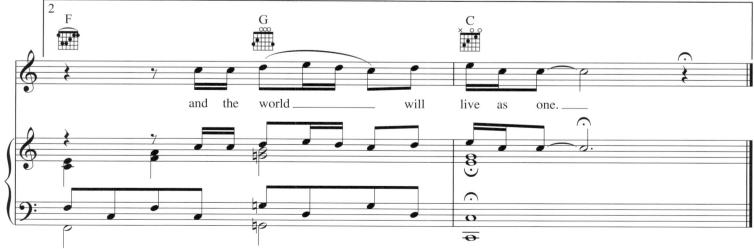

and the world _____ will live as one. ___

IN MY LIFE

Words and Music by JOHN LENNON
and PAUL McCARTNEY

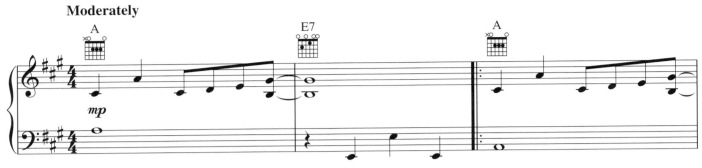

There are plac - es I'll re - mem - ber all my
But of all these friends and lov - ers there is

life, _____ though some have changed. _ Some for - ev - er, not for
no _____ one com - pares with you. _ And these mem - 'ries lose their

bet - ter; some have gone _____ and some re - main. _ All these
mean - ing when I think of _ love as some - thing new. _ Tho' I

(1.) plac - es ___ had ___ their ___ mo - ments   with lov - ers and friends ___ I
(2.,3.) know ___ I'll ___ nev - er lose af - fec - tion   for peo - ple and things ___ that

still can re - call. ___   Some are dead ___ and ___ some ___ are ___
went ___ be - fore, ___   I know I'll of - ten stop and think a -

To Coda ⊕

liv - ing, ___   in my ___ life I've loved them all. ___
bout them, ___   in my ___ life I love you more. ___

In 18th century style

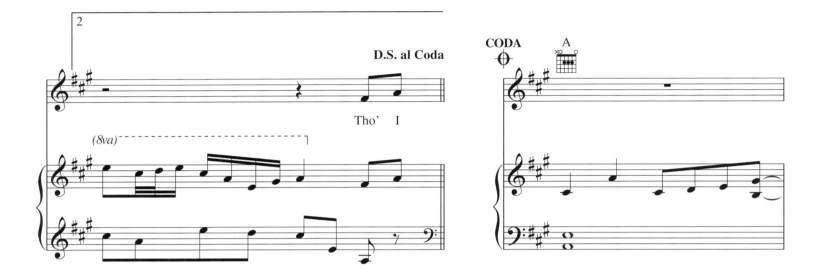

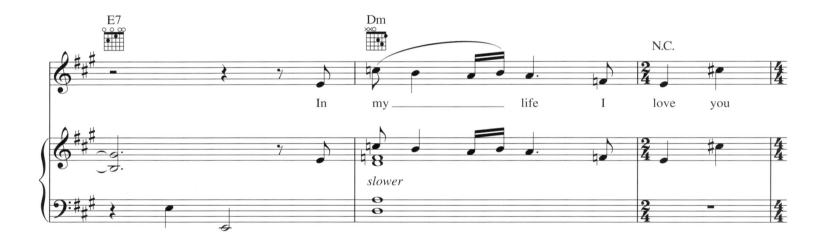

LET IT BE

Words and Music by JOHN LENNON
and PAUL McCARTNEY

When I find my-self __ in times of trou-ble

Instrumental

Moth-er Mar-y comes to me speak-ing words of wis-dom; let it

be. __ And in my hour of dark-ness, she is

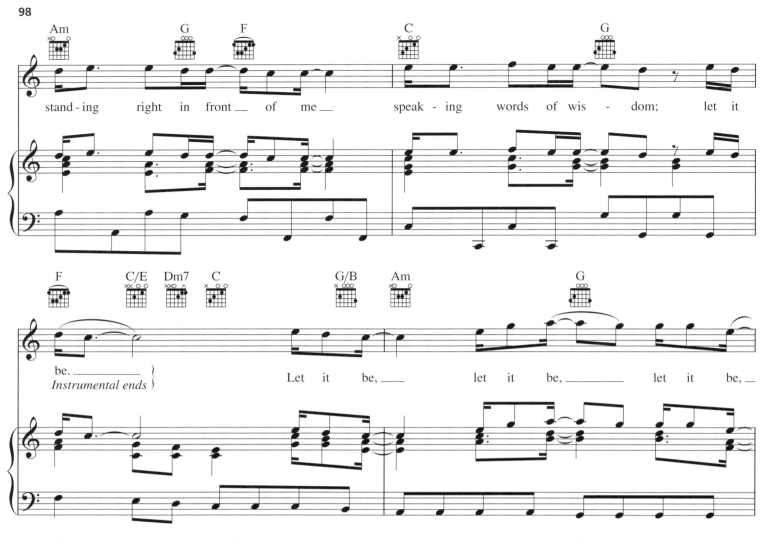

stand-ing right in front __ of me __ speak-ing words of wis - dom; let it

be. _____

Instrumental ends

Let it be, __ let it be, _____ let it be, __

_____ let it be. _____ Whis-per words __ of wis - dom; let it be. __

{ And when __ the bro-ken - heart - ed peo - ple
{ And when __ the night __ is cloud - y, there is

let it be. _____ There will be ___ an an - swer; let it be. ___

Let it be, ___ let it be, _____ let it be, ___

let it be. ___

{ Whis - per words ___ of wis - dom; let it be. __
{ There will be _____ an an - swer; let it be. __

To Coda ⊕

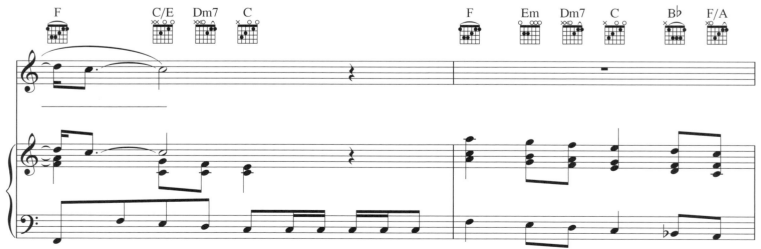

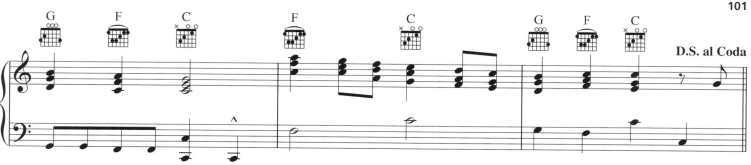

D.S. al Coda

Let it be, ____ let it be, ____ let it be, ____

_____ let it be. ____ Whis- per words __ of wis - dom; let it be. __

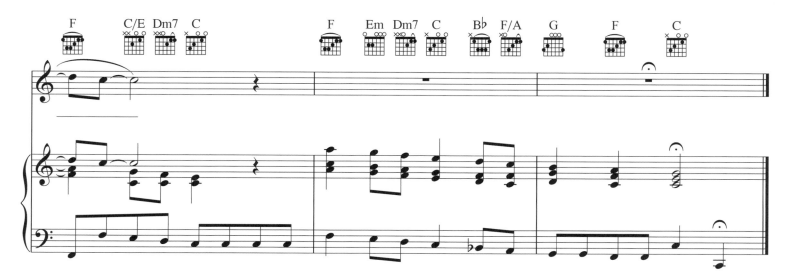

A MOMENT LIKE THIS

Words and Music by JOHN REID
and JORGEN KJELL ELOFSSON

Moderately slow

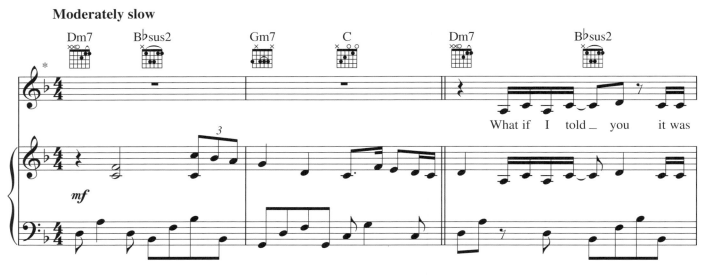

What if I told ___ you it was

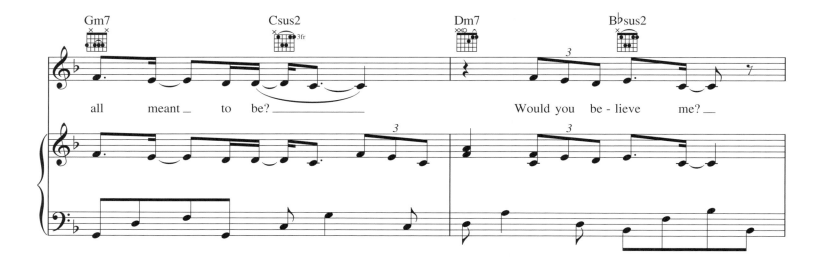

all meant ___ to be? _____ Would you be - lieve me? ___

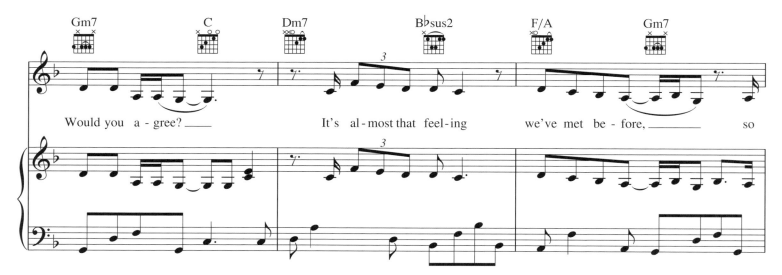

Would you a - gree? ___ It's al - most that feel-ing we've met be - fore, _____ so

* Recorded a half step lower.

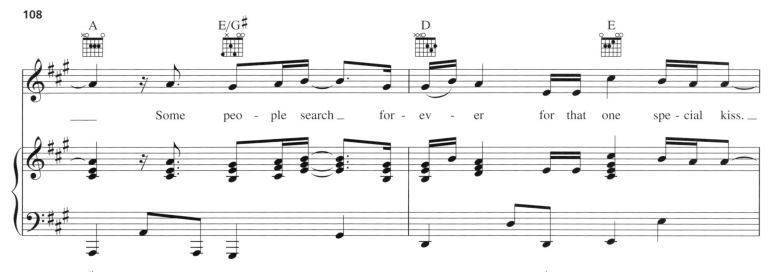

Some peo-ple search___ for-ev-er for that one spe-cial kiss.___

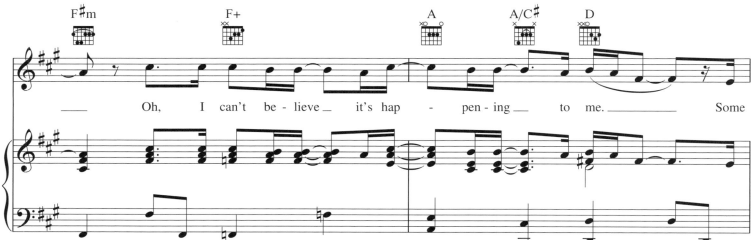

___ Oh, I can't be-lieve___ it's hap-pen-ing___ to me._____ Some

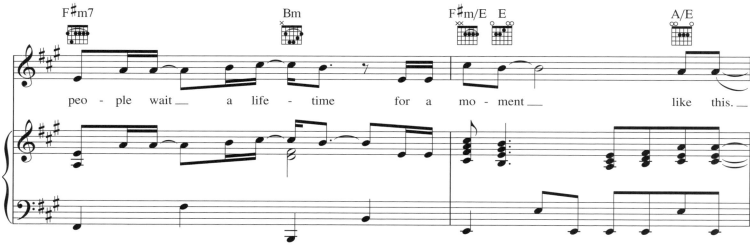

peo-ple wait___ a life-time for a mo-ment___ like this.___

Choir: (Mo-ment like this.) ___
Lead vocal ad lib.

A NEW DAY HAS COME

Words and Music by STEPHAN MOCCIO
and ALDO NOVA

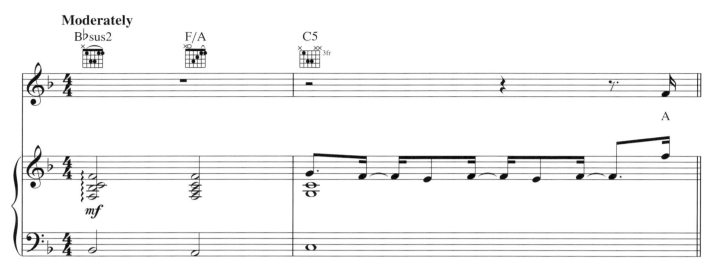

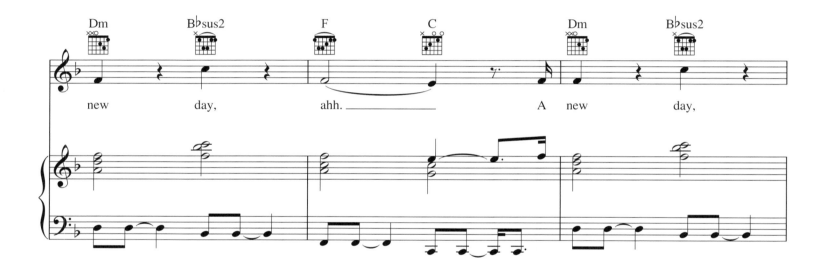

Original key: F♯ major. This edition has been transposed down one half-step to be more playable.

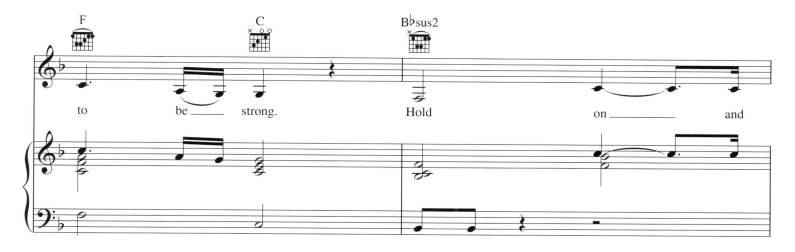

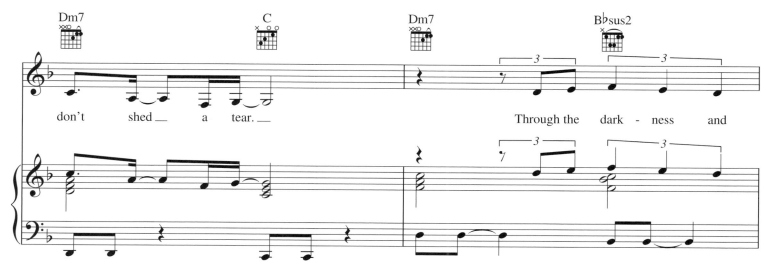

way my tears. _____ Let it fill my soul and drown my

fears. _____ Let it shat-ter the walls for a

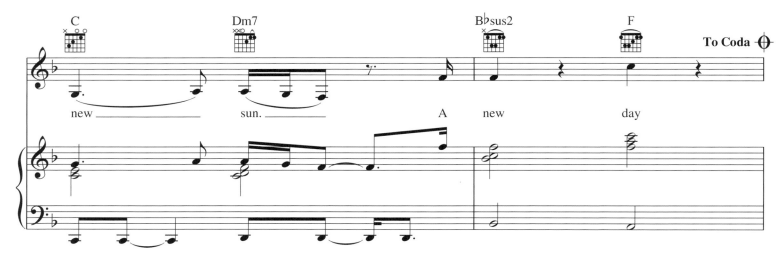

new _____ sun. _____ A new day

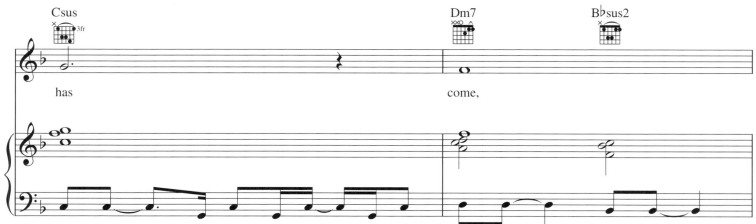

has come,

found my strength all in _____ the

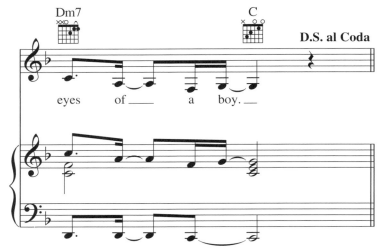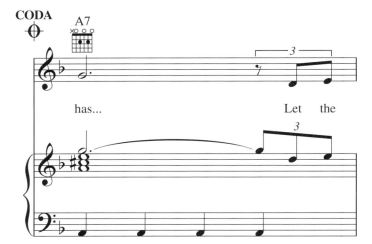

eyes of ___ a boy. ___   **D.S. al Coda**   **CODA** has...   Let the

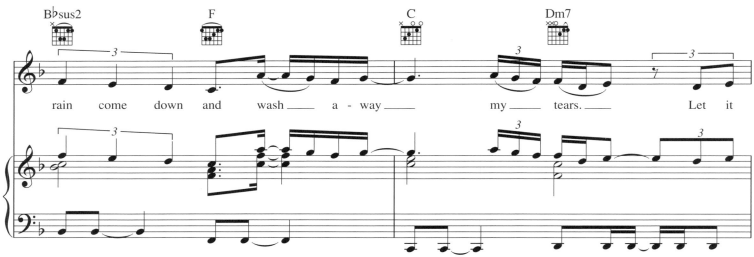

rain come down and wash ___ a - way ___ my ___ tears. ___ Let it

fill my soul and drown my fears. _____ Let it

shat - ter the walls for a new _____ sun. _____ A

new day has _____

_____ come, oh, _____ la, la, _

_____ oh. _____

I can't _ be - lieve _ I've _ been touched by _ an an - gel _ with

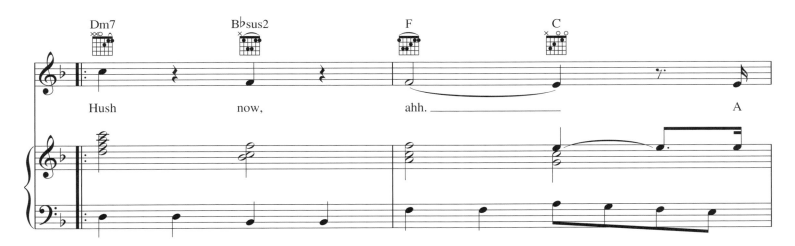

love, _____ ooh. _____

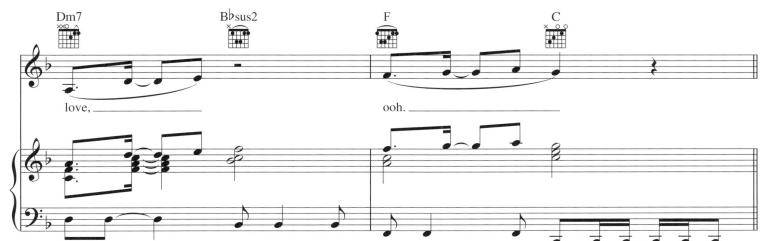

Hush now, ahh. _____ A

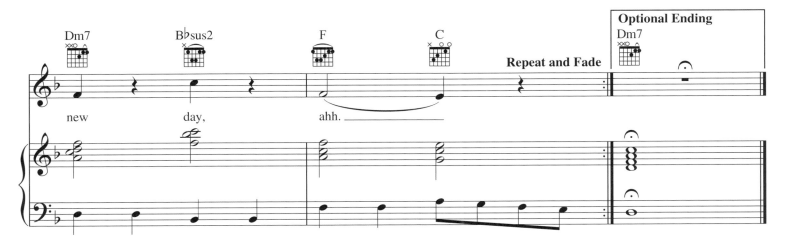

new day, ahh. _____

Repeat and Fade

Optional Ending

100 YEARS

Words and Music by
JOHN ONDRASIK

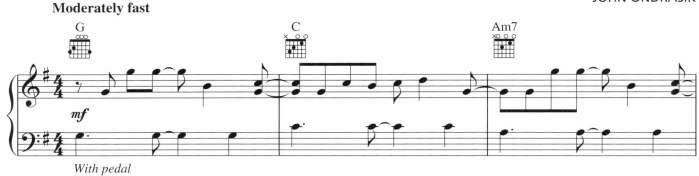

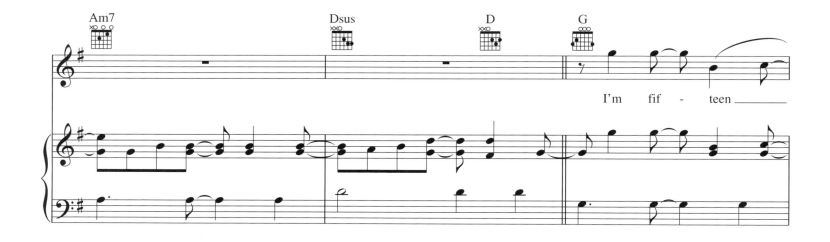

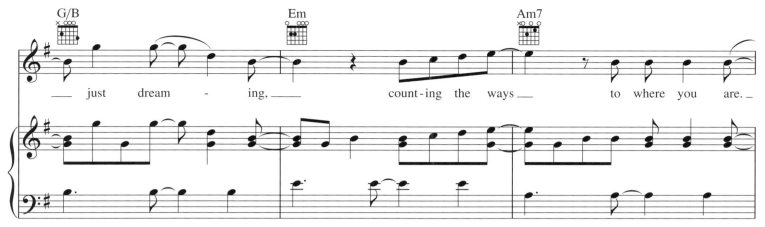

just dream - ing, ____ count-ing the ways ____ to where you are. __

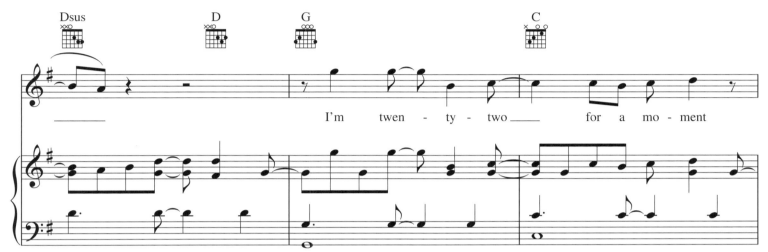

____ I'm twen-ty-two ____ for a mo-ment

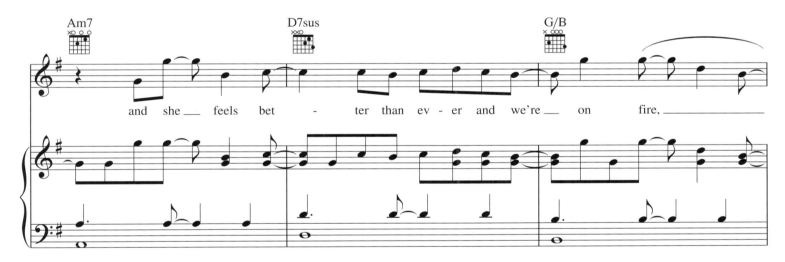

and she ____ feels bet - ter than ev-er and we're ____ on fire, _____

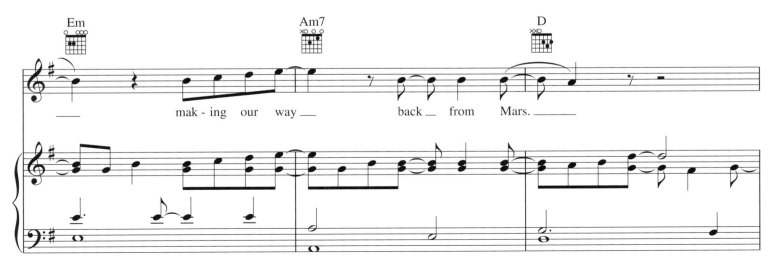

____ mak-ing our way ____ back ____ from Mars. _____

Fif - teen, there's ___ still time ___ for you. ___ Time ___ to buy ___

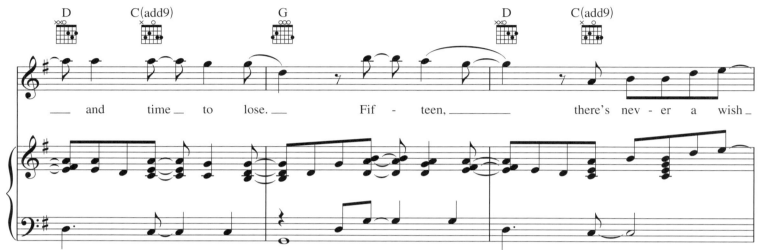

___ and time ___ to lose. ___ Fif - teen, ___ there's nev - er a wish ___

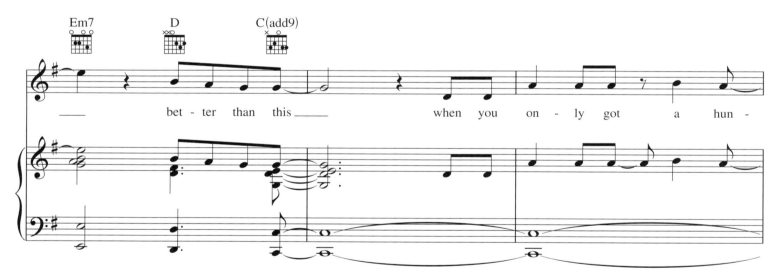

___ bet - ter than this ___ when you on - ly got a hun -

- dred years to live. ___

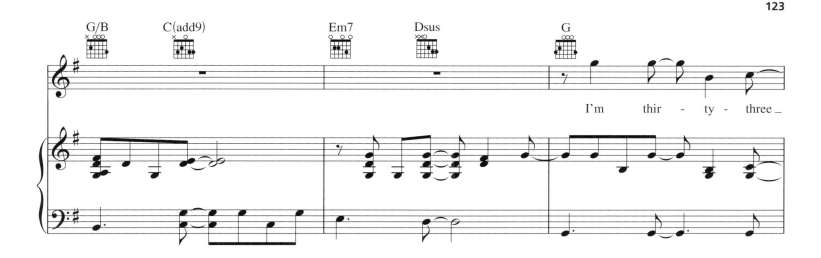

I'm thir - ty - three

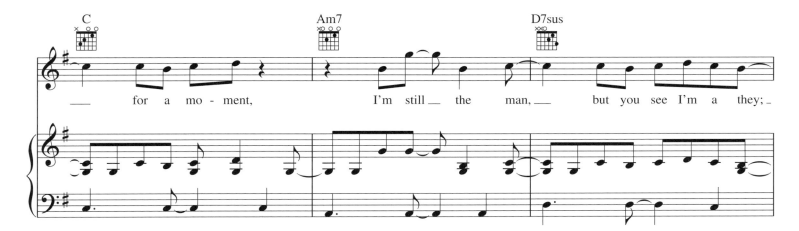

for a mo - ment, I'm still the man, but you see I'm a they;

a kid on the way, a fam - 'ly on my mind.

I'm for - ty - five for a mo - ment,

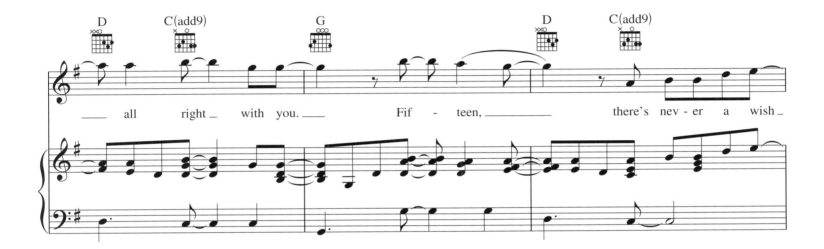

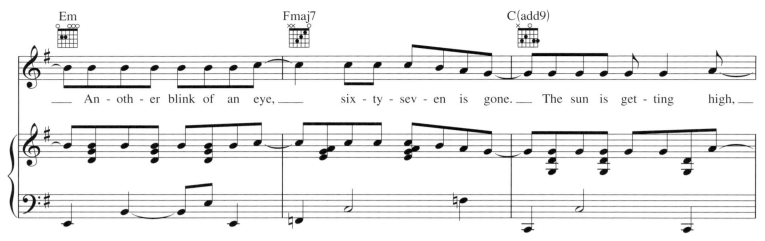

An - oth - er blink of an eye, ____ six - ty - sev - en is gone. ____ The sun is get - ting high, ____

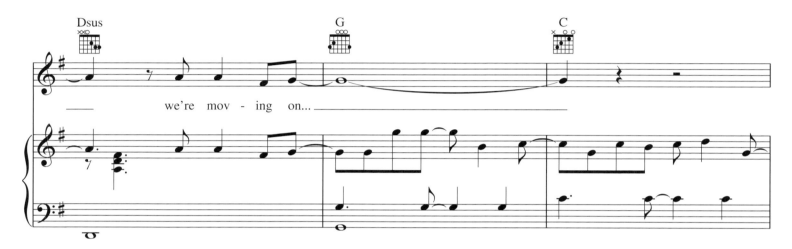

____ we're mov - ing on... ____

I'm nine - ty - nine ____

____ for a mo - ment, I'm dying ____ for just ____ an - oth - er mo - ment and I'm ____

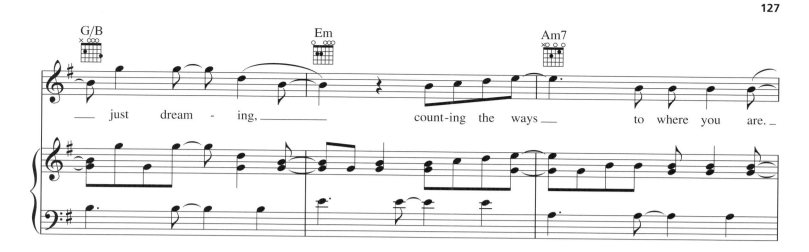

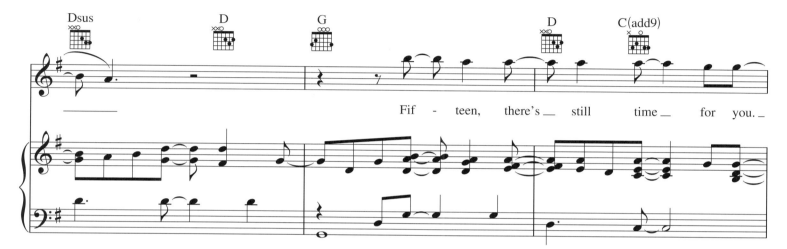

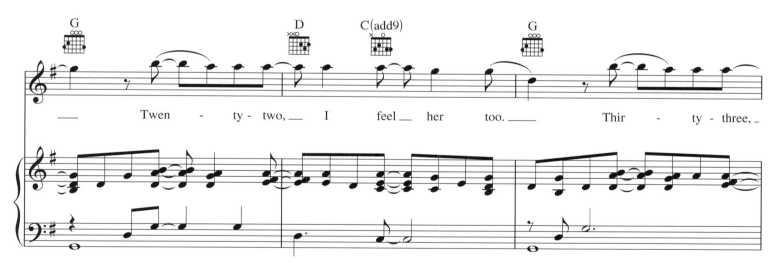

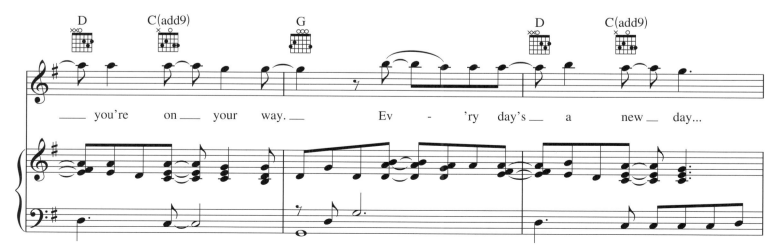

Hey, fif - teen, there's nev - er a wish _____ bet - ter than this _____

_____ when you on - ly got _____ a hun - dred years to live. _____

rit.

ONLY HOPE

from the Warner Bros. Motion Picture A WALK TO REMEMBER

Words and Music by
JONATHAN FOREMAN

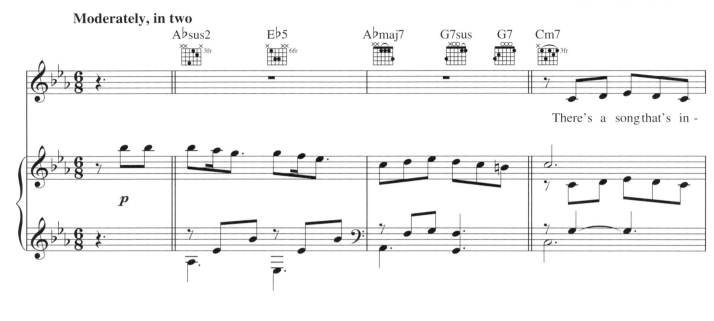

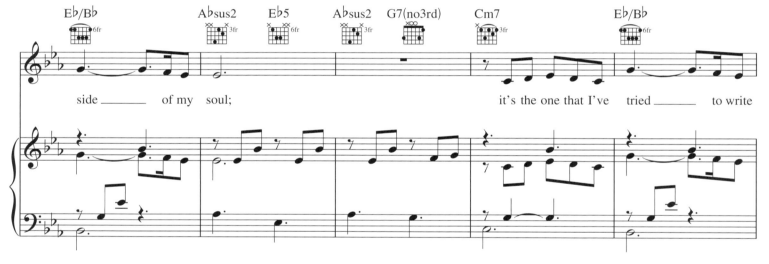

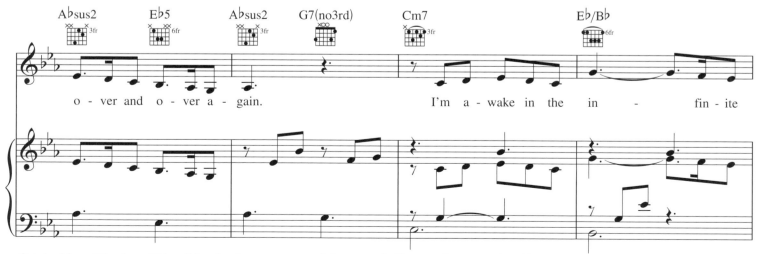

Original key: C# minor. This edition has been transposed down one half-step to be more playable.

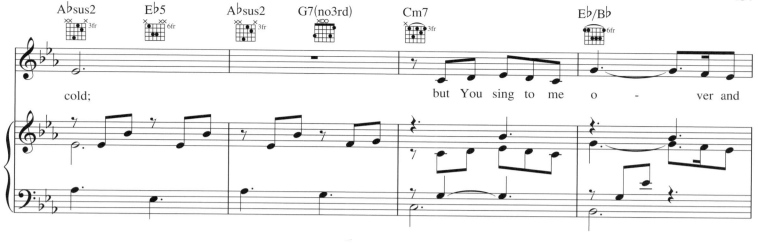

cold;　　　　　　　　　but You sing to me o - ver and

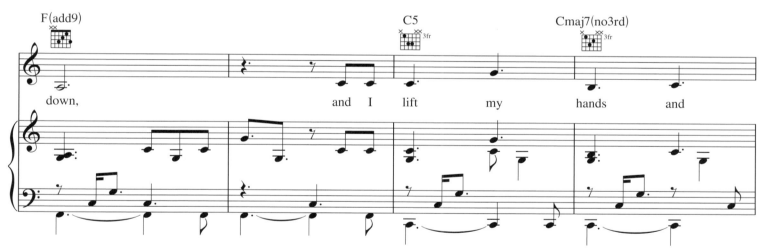

o - ver and o - ver a - gain.　So I　lay　my　head　back

cresc.　　*mf*

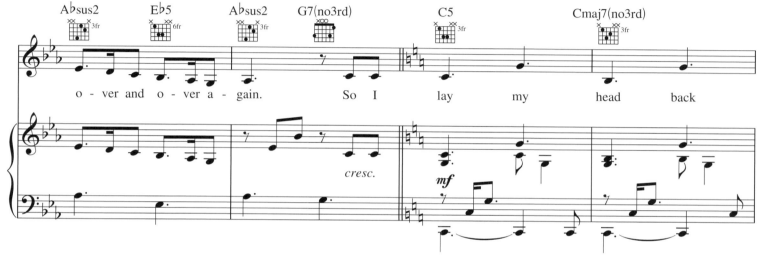

down,　　　　　and I　lift　my　hands　and

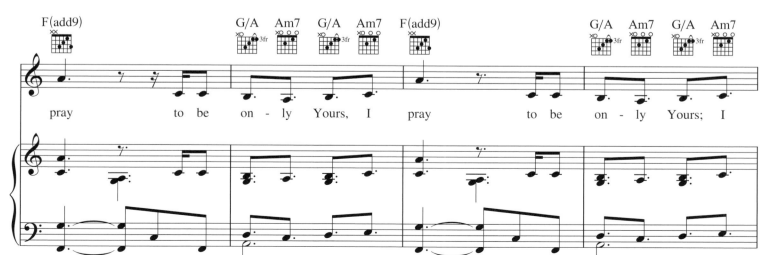

pray　　　to　be　on - ly　Yours, I　pray　　to　be　on - ly　Yours; I

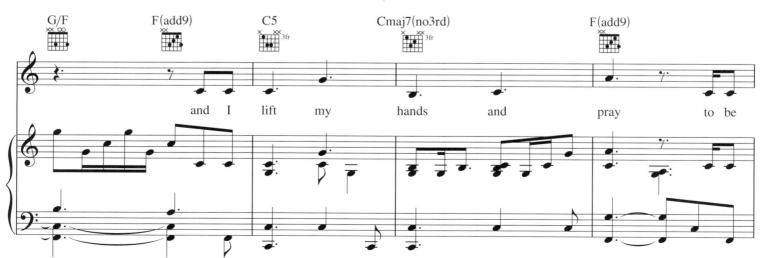

OUR HOUSE

Words and Music by
GRAHAM NASH

Moderately slow

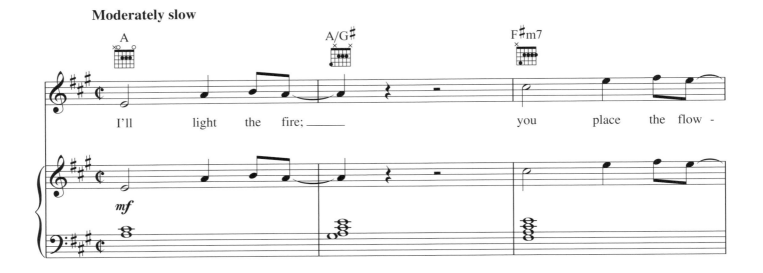

I'll light the fire; _____ you place the flow-

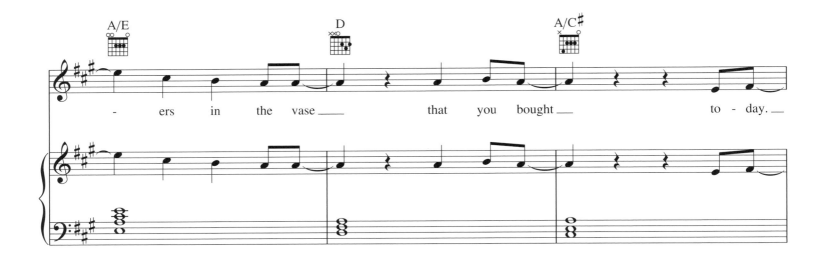

-ers in the vase _____ that you bought _____ to - day. _____

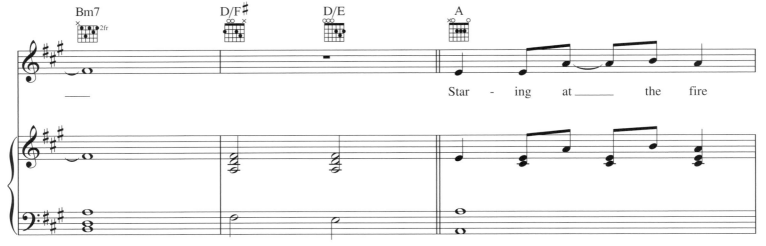

_____ Star-ing at _____ the fire

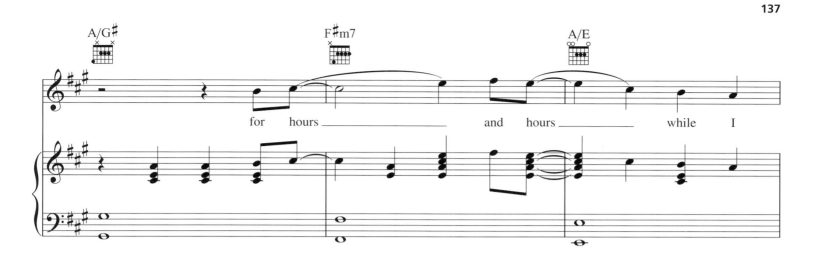

for hours _____ and hours _____ while I

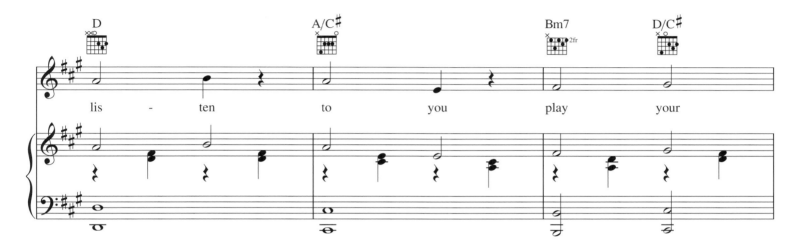

lis - ten to you play your

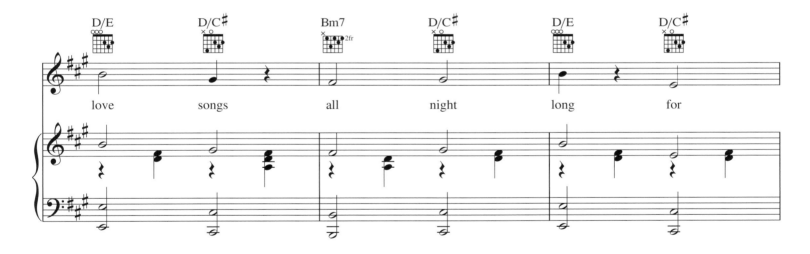

love songs all night long for

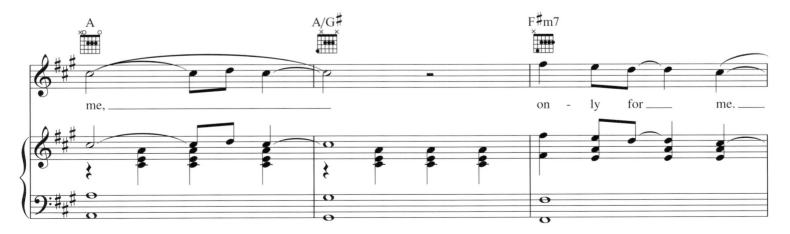

me, _____ on - ly for _____ me. _____

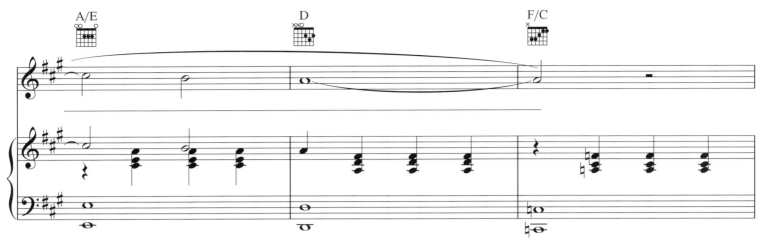

Come to me now _____ and rest _____ your head _____ for just _____
(Come to me now.) _____

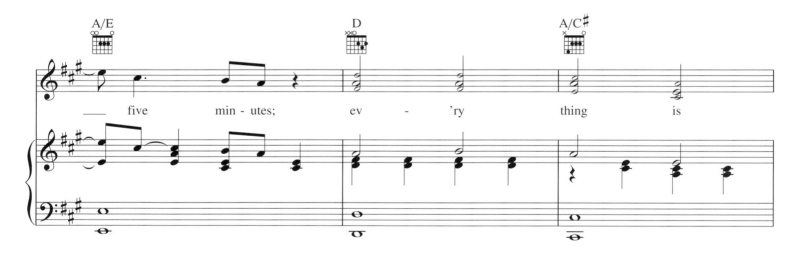

_____ five min - utes; ev - 'ry thing is

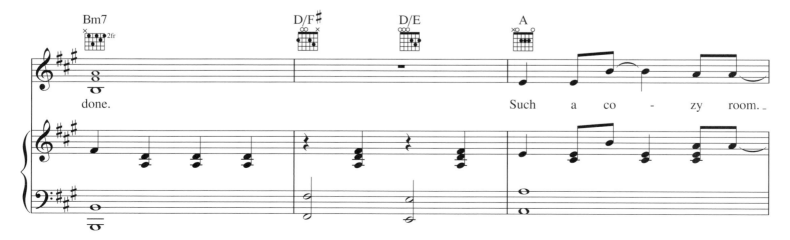

done. Such a co - zy room. _

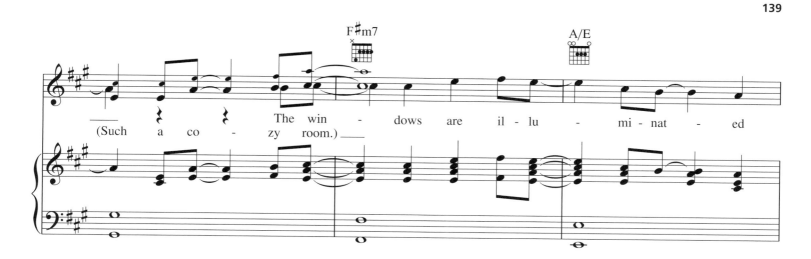

(Such a co - zy room.) ___ The win - dows are il - lu - mi - nat - ed

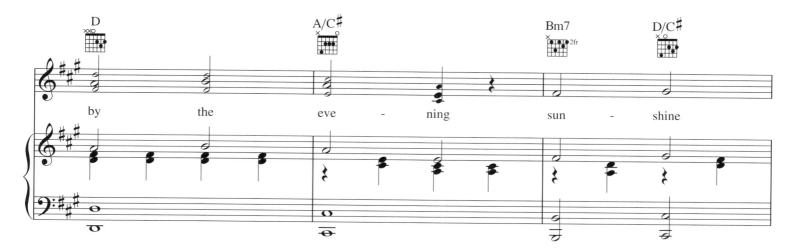

by the eve - ning sun - shine

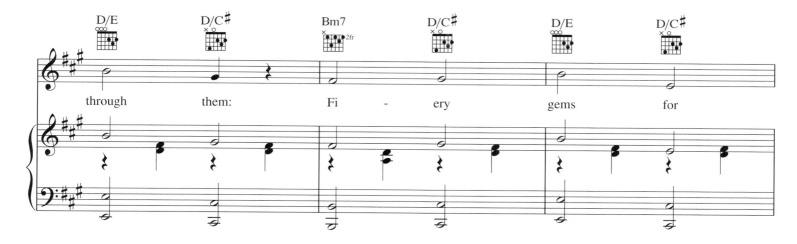

through them: Fi - ery gems for

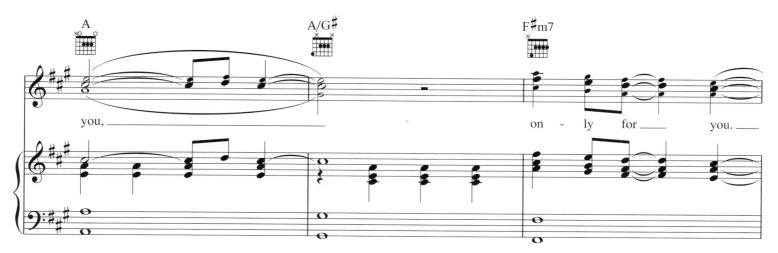

you, ___ on - ly for ___ you. ___

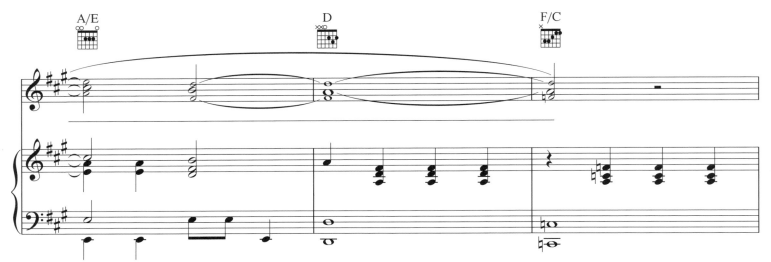

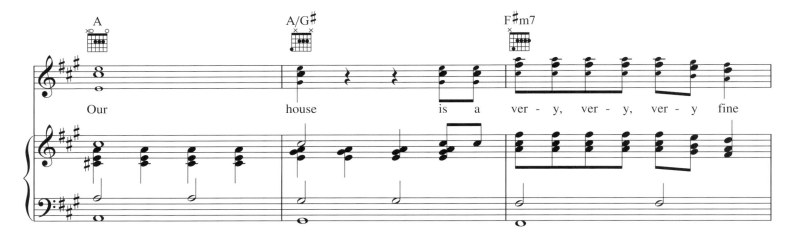

Our house is a ver-y, ver-y, ver-y fine

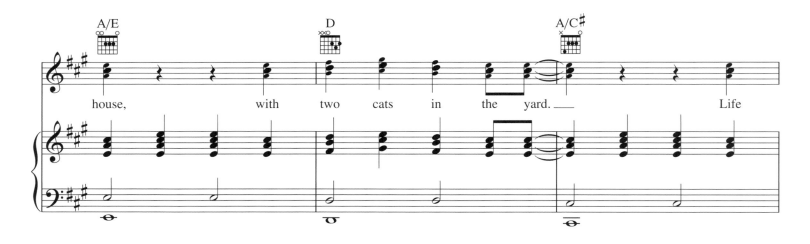

house, with two cats in the yard. ____ Life

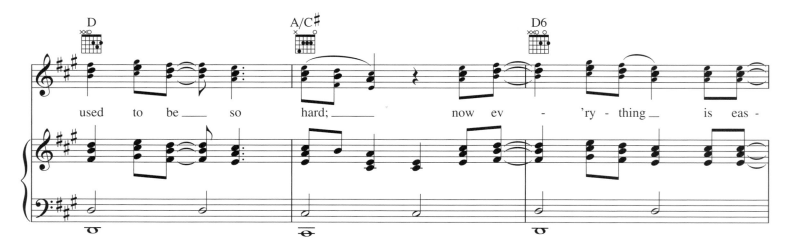

used to be ____ so hard; ____ now ev-'ry-thing ____ is eas-

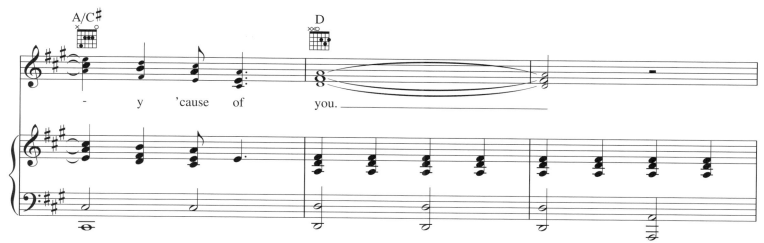

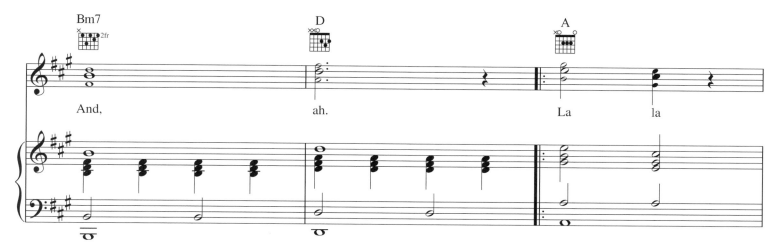

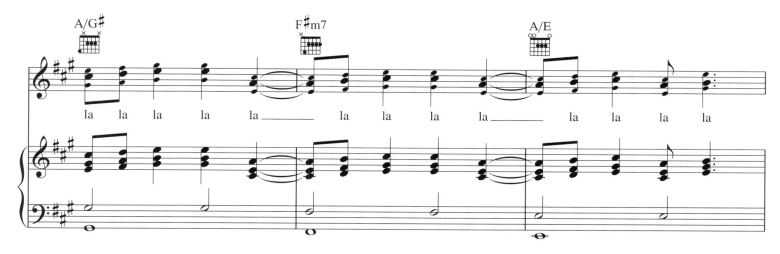

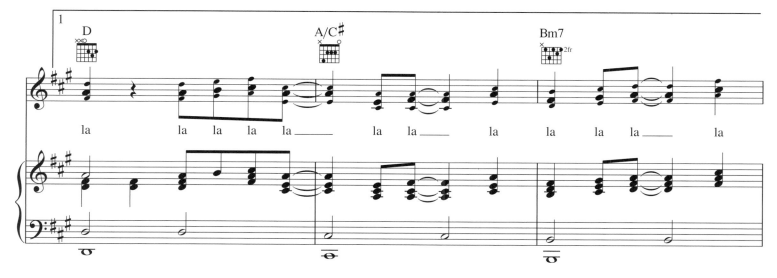

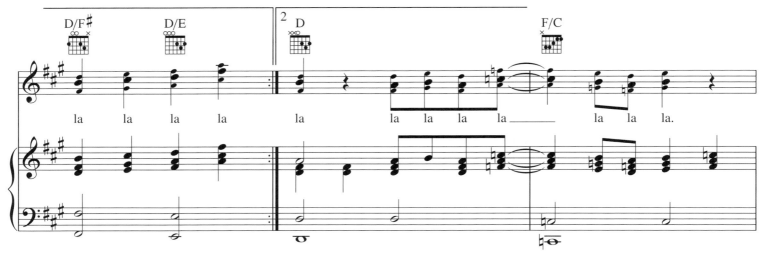

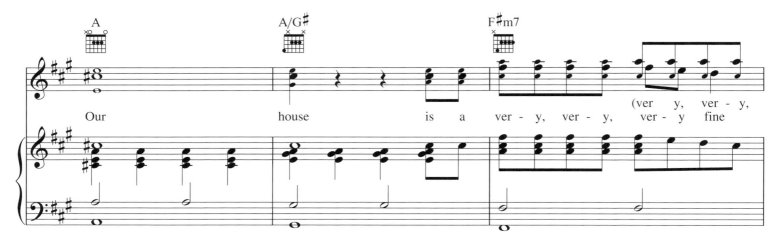

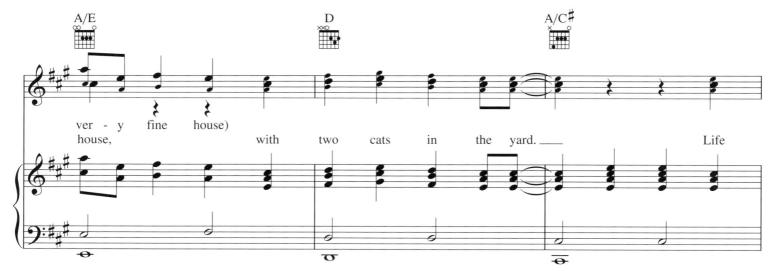

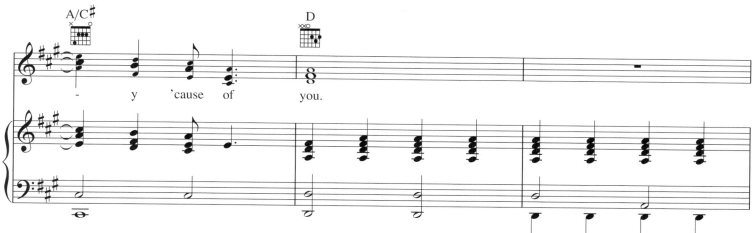

-y 'cause of you.

Slowly

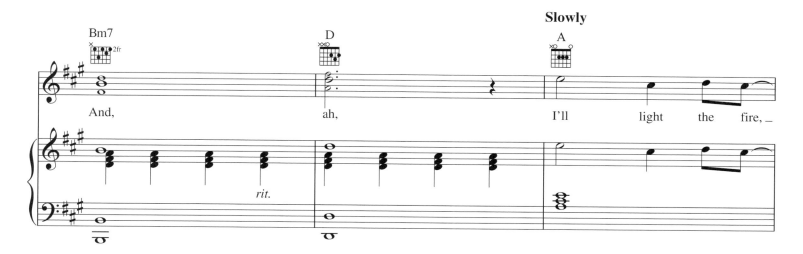

And, ah, I'll light the fire, __

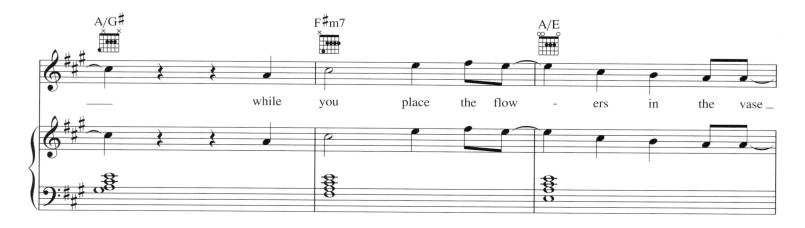

__ while you place the flow - ers in the vase __

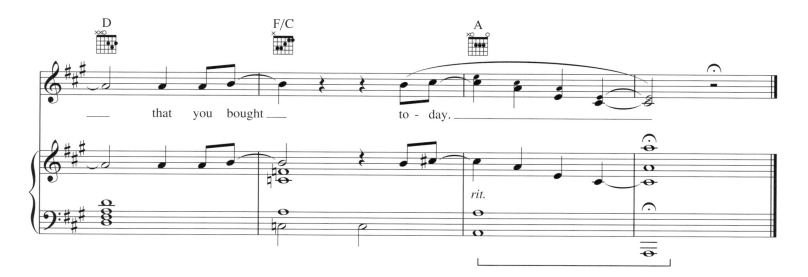

__ that you bought __ to - day. __

REACH OUT AND TOUCH
(Somebody's Hand)

Words and Music by NICKOLAS ASHFORD
and VALERIE SIMPSON

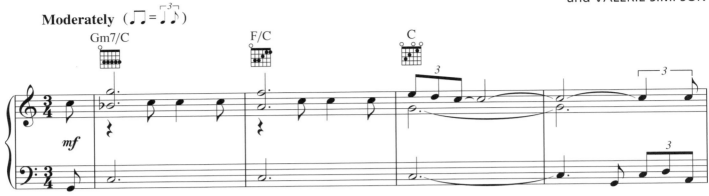

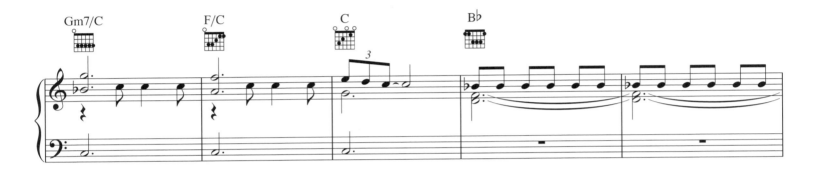

Reach out and touch some-bod-y's hand. Make this world a

bet-ter place if you can. Reach out and touch

some - bod - y's hand. Make this world a bet - ter place if you

can. Just try. {Take a lit - tle time out of your bus - y day to
If you see an old friend on the street and he's

give en - cour - age - ment to some - one who's lost the way.
down, re - mem - ber his shoes could fit your feet.

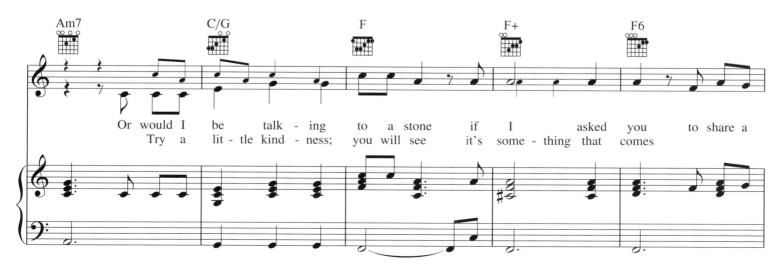

Or would I be talk - ing to a stone if I asked you to share a
Try a lit - tle kind - ness; you will see it's some - thing that comes

prob - lem   that's not your own? _____
ver - y nat - 'ral   -   ly. _____

We   can

change _ things   if we start giv - ing.   Why don't you reach out and   Why don't you,

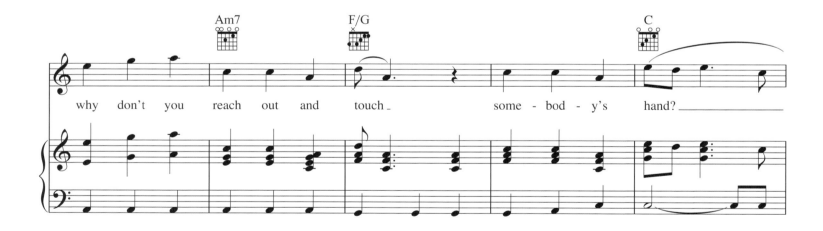

why don't you reach out and touch _   some - bod - y's hand? _____

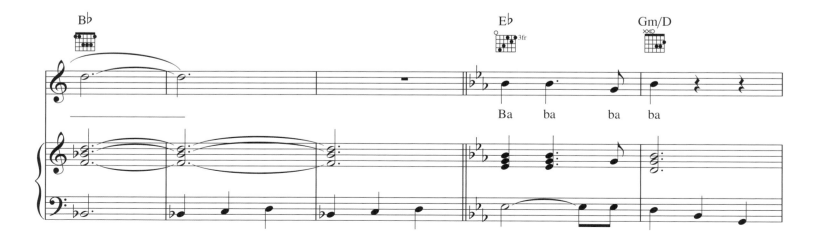

Ba   ba   ba   ba

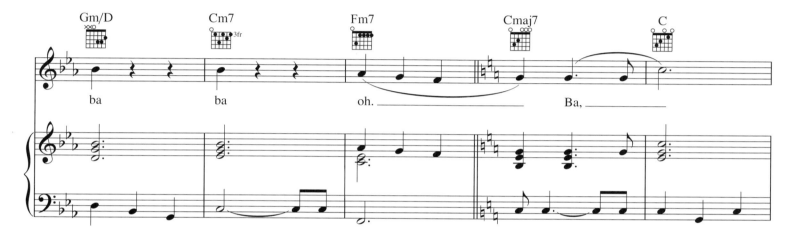

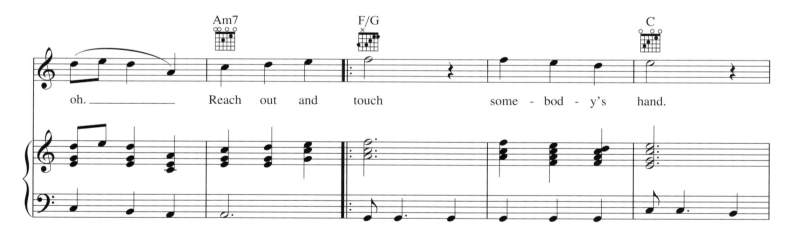

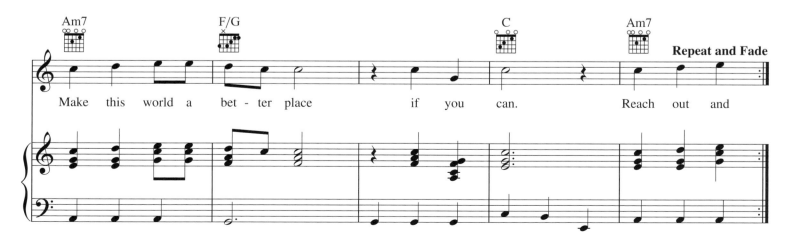

SEASONS OF LOVE

from RENT

Words and Music by
JONATHAN LARSON

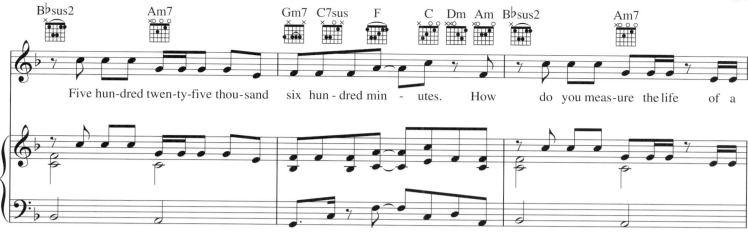

Bbsus2 — Am7 — Gm7 C7sus F — C Dm Am Bbsus2 — Am7

Five hun-dred twen-ty-five thou-sand six hun-dred min - utes. How do you meas-ure the life of a

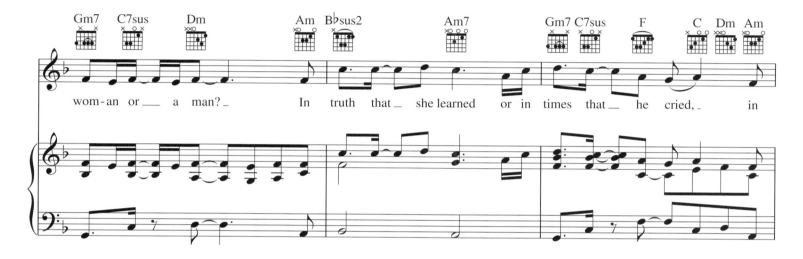

Gm7 C7sus Dm — Am Bbsus2 — Am7 — Gm7 C7sus F — C Dm Am

wom-an or ___ a man? ___ In truth that ___ she learned or in times that ___ he cried, ___ in

Bbsus2 — Am7 — Gm7 C7sus Dm — Am Bbsus2 — Am7

bridg - es ___ he burned or the way that she died. _____ It's time now to sing out, though the

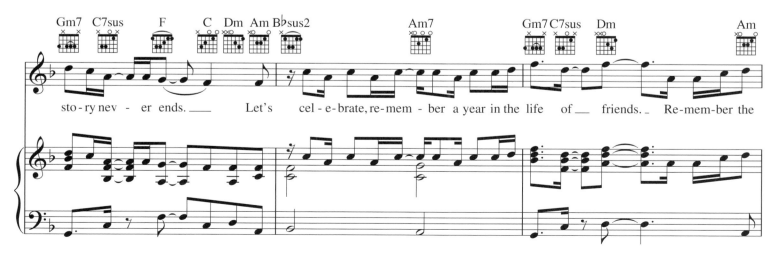

Gm7 C7sus F — C Dm Am Bbsus2 — Am7 — Gm7 C7sus Dm — Am

sto - ry nev - er ends. ___ Let's cel - e - brate, re-mem - ber a year in the life of ___ friends. ___ Re-mem-ber the

SOMEWHERE OUT THERE
from AN AMERICAN TAIL

Music by BARRY MANN
and JAMES HORNER
Lyrics by CYNTHIA WEIL

Moderately, with expression

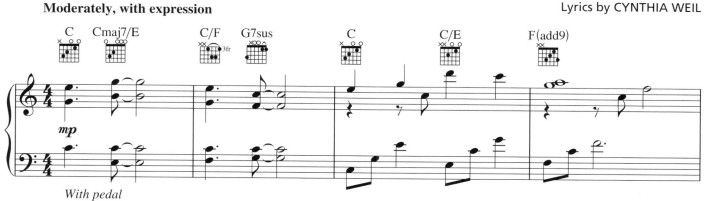

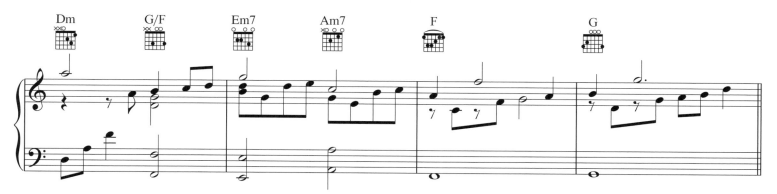

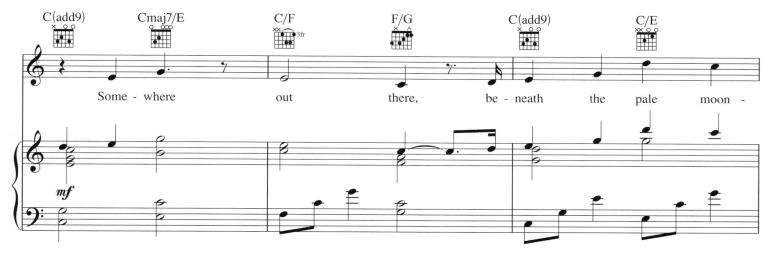

Some - where out there, be - neath the pale moon -

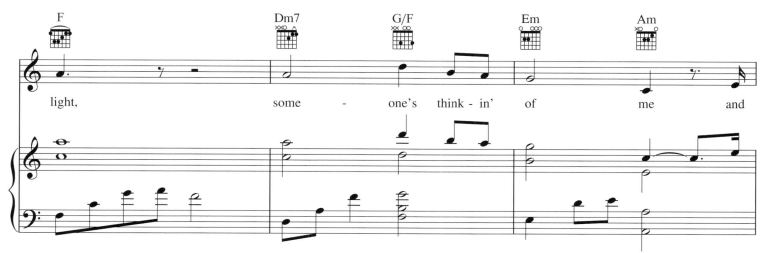

light, some - one's think - in' of me and

lov - ing me to - night. Some - where out ___

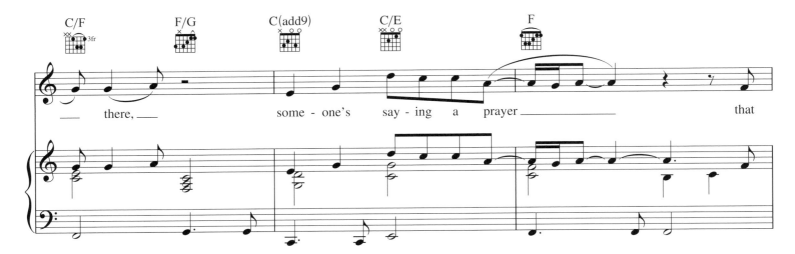

___ there, ___ some - one's say - ing a prayer _____ that

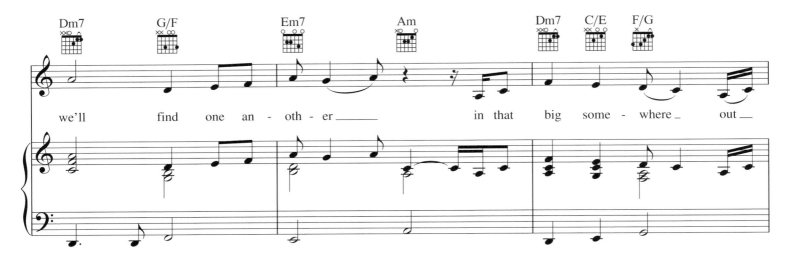

we'll find one an - oth - er _____ in that big some - where ___ out ___

there. And e - ven though I know how ver - y far a - part ___ we are _____ it

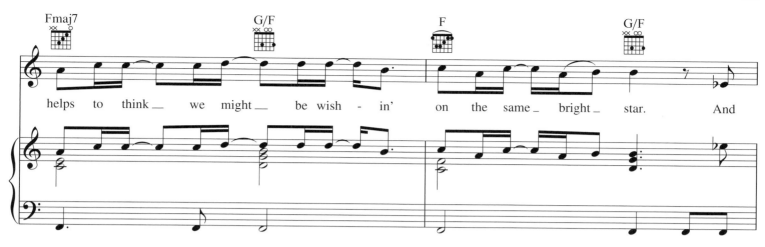

helps to think __ we might __ be wish - in' on the same __ bright __ star. And

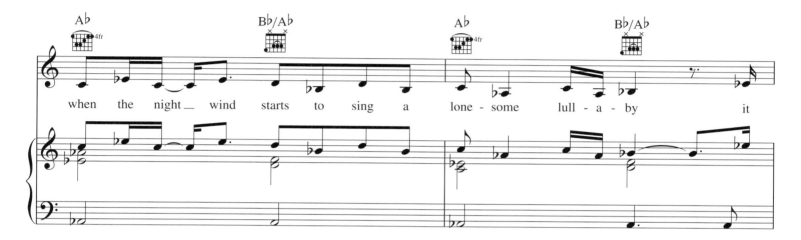

when the night __ wind starts to sing a lone - some lull - a - by it

helps to think we're sleep - ing un - der - neath the same big sky.

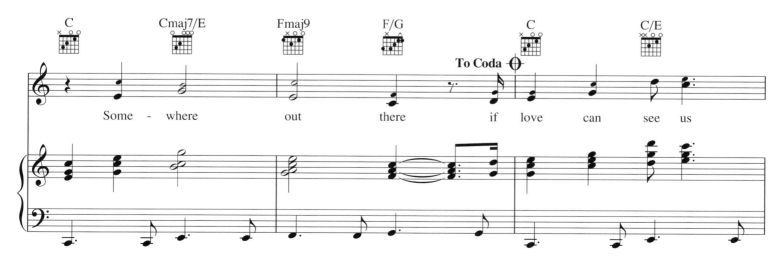

To Coda

Some - where out there if love can see us

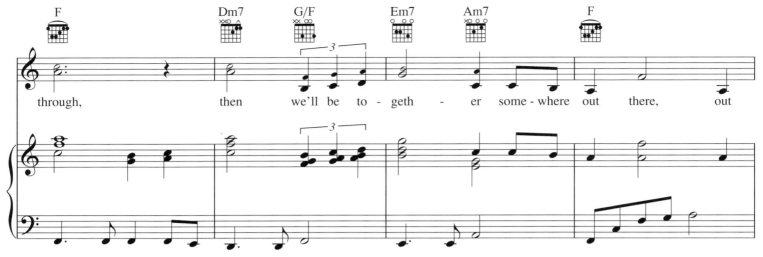

through, then we'll be to- geth - er some-where out there, out

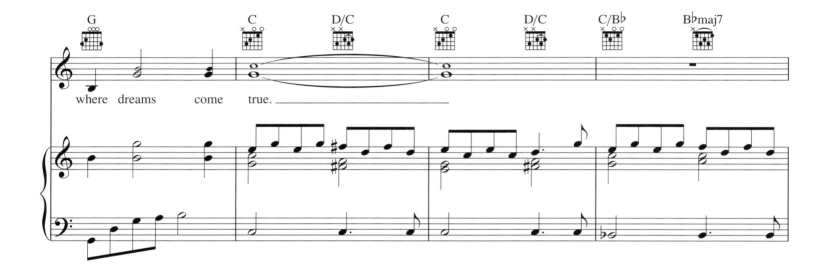

where dreams come true. _____

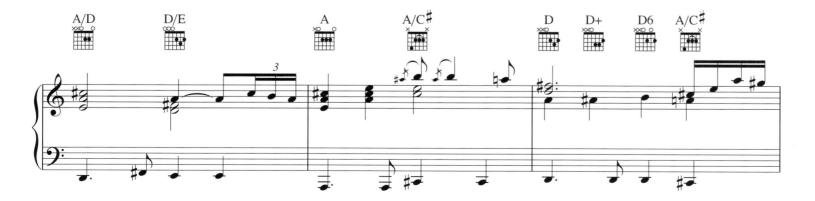

D.S. al Coda

And

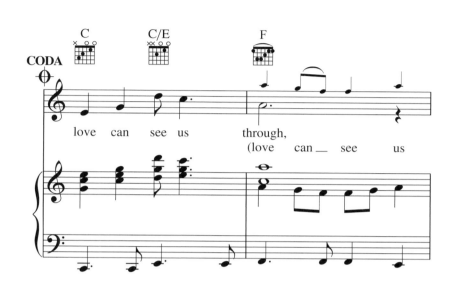

CODA

love can see us through, (love can see us

then we'll be to- geth - er some- where out there, out where dreams come
through)

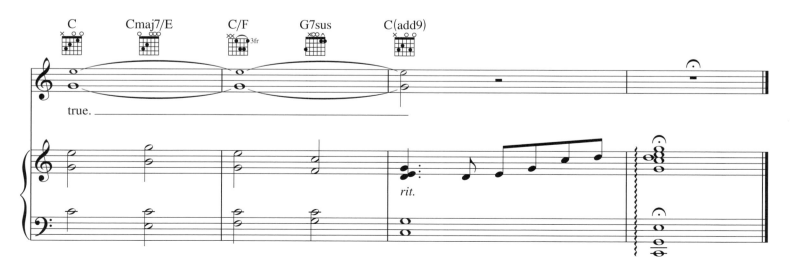

true. _____

STAND BY ME

Words and Music by JERRY LEIBER,
MIKE STOLLER and BEN E. KING

Moderately, with a beat

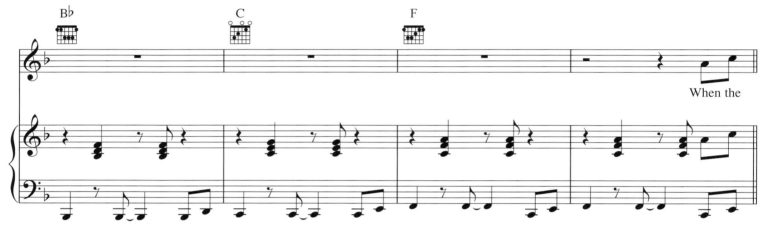

When the

night ___ has come ___ and the land is
sky ___ that we look up - on ___ should tum - ble and

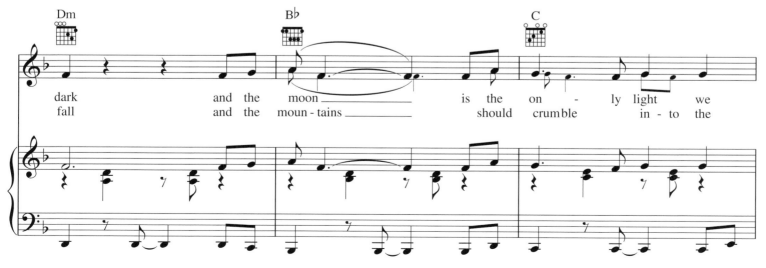

dark ___ and the moon ___ is the on - ly light we
fall ___ and the moun - tains ___ should crumble in - to the

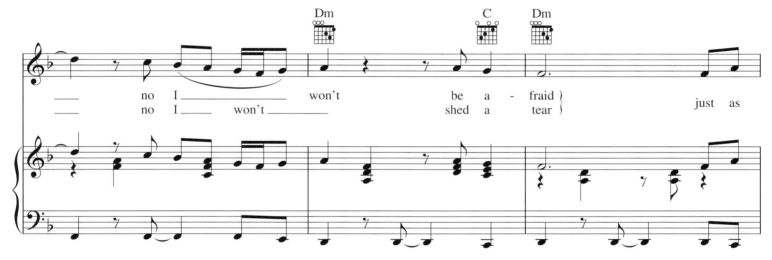

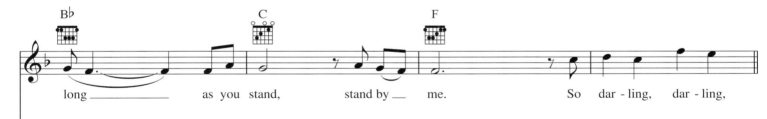

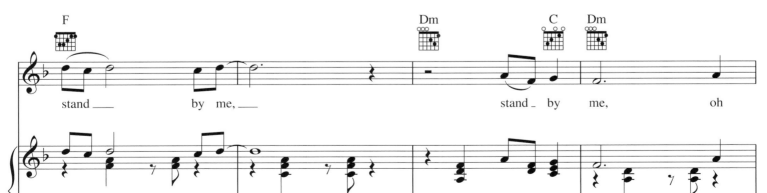

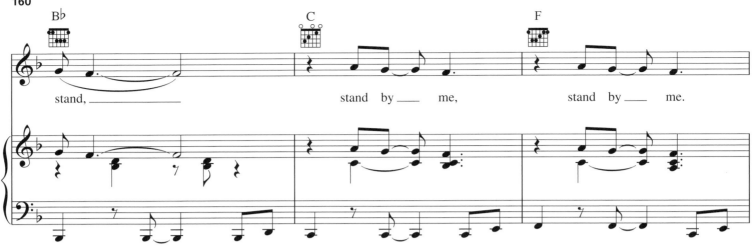

stand, _____ stand by ___ me, stand by ___ me.

If the ___ Dar-ling, stand _____ by me, _

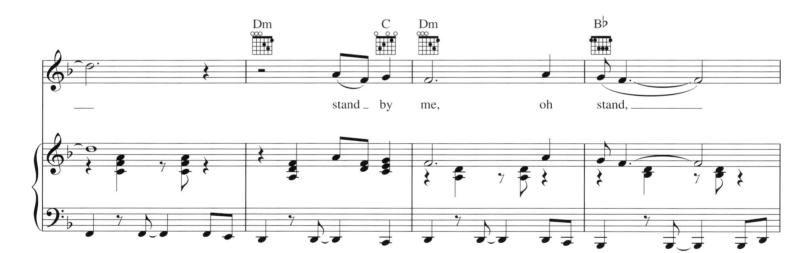

___ stand _ by _ me, oh stand, _____

Repeat and Fade

stand by ___ me, stand by ___ me. When-ev-er I'm in trou-ble won't you

THERE YOU'LL BE

from Touchstone Pictures'/Jerry Bruckheimer Films' PEARL HARBOR

Words and Music by
DIANE WARREN

Slowly, steadily

When I think back on ___ these times ___ and the
showed me how ___ it feels ___ to feel the

dreams we left ___ be-hind, ___ I'll be glad, 'cause I ___ was blessed to get, ___ to
sky with-in ___ my reach, ___ and I al-ways will ___ re-mem-ber all ___ the

have you in my life. ___ When I look back on ___ these days ___ I'll ___
strength you gave to me. ___ Your love made me make ___ it through; ___ oh ___ I

-'ry - where __ I am, __ there you'll be, _____ and ev-

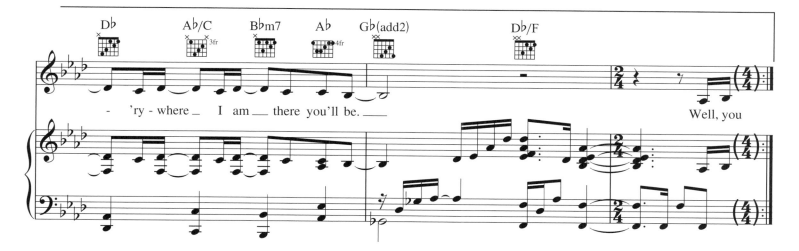

-'ry - where __ I am __ there you'll be. ____ Well, you

__ I'll keep __ a part ____ of you __ with me, ____ and ev-

-'ry - where __ I am, __ there you'll be. ____ 'Cause I al-ways saw in you __ my light, __

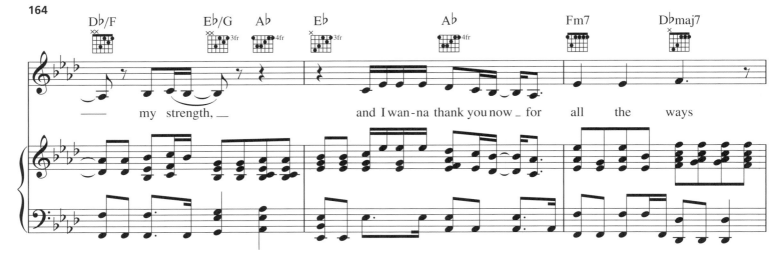

my strength, ___ and I wan-na thank you now ___ for all the ways

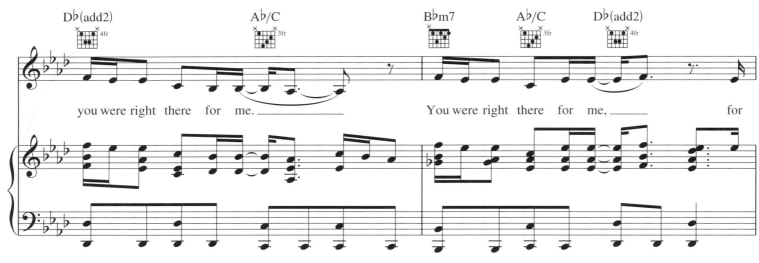

you were right there for me. _____ You were right there for me, _____ for

al - ways. _____ In my dreams I'll al - ways see you

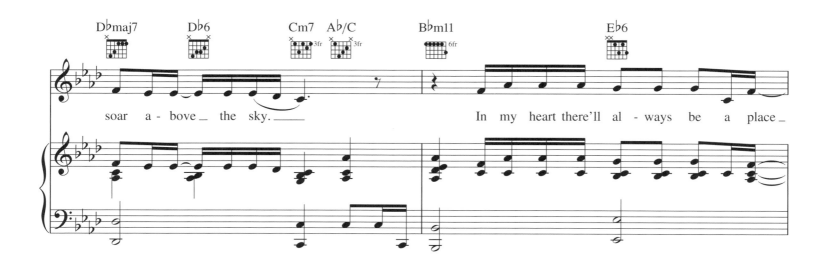

soar a - bove ___ the sky. _____ In my heart there'll al - ways be a place ___

for you for all ___ my life. _____ I'll keep ___ a part ___

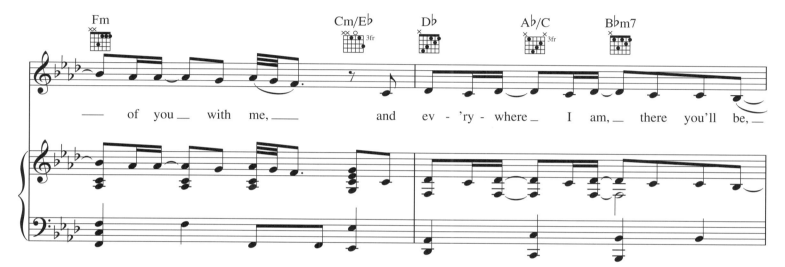

___ of you ___ with me, ___ and ev - 'ry - where ___ I am, ___ there you'll be, ___

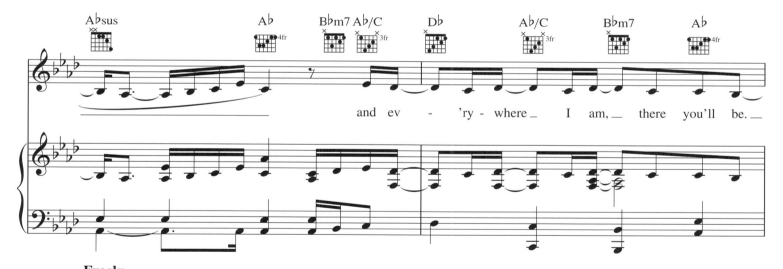

and ev - 'ry - where ___ I am, ___ there you'll be. ___

Freely

There you'll be. _____

THROUGH THE YEARS

Words and Music by STEVE DORFF
and MARTY PANZER

Appreciatively

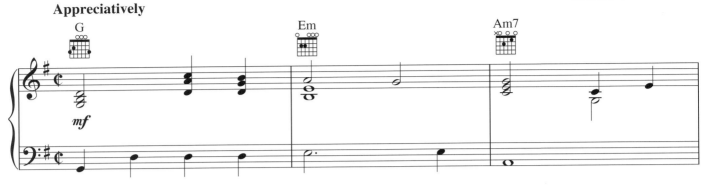

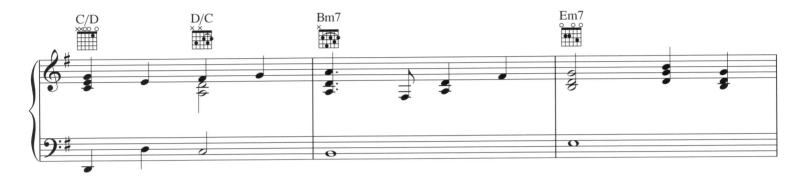

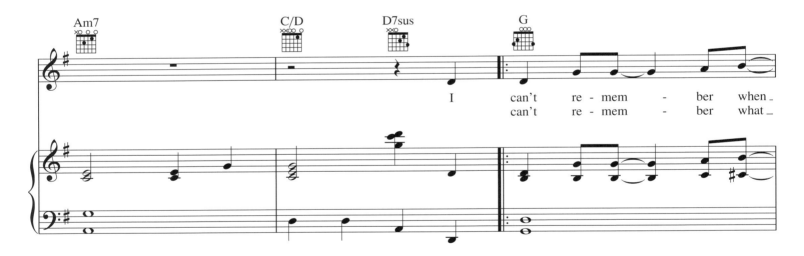

I can't re-mem-ber when _____
can't re-mem-ber what _____

_____ you were -n't there, _____
_____ I used _____ to do, _____

when I did -n't care _____
who I trust -ed, who _____

made.   And   I'm _____ so glad I've stayed _____

way.   As   long _____ as it's o - kay _____

_____ right here with you _____   through   the

_____ I'll stay with you _____   through   the

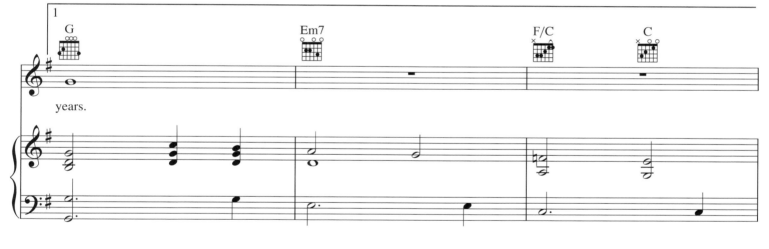

years.

I   years.

TRUE COLORS

Words and Music by BILLY STEINBERG
and TOM KELLY

Relaxed tempo

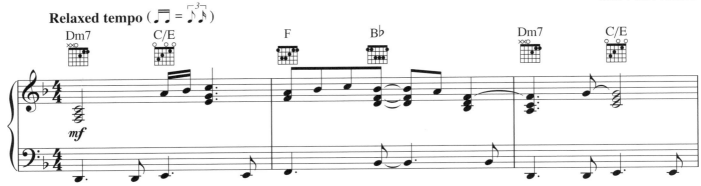

You with the

sad   eyes,   don't be dis-cour-aged. Oh, I re-al-ize   it's
smile   then,   don't be un-hap-py. Can't re-mem-ber when   I

hard   to take cour-age.   In   a   world   full   of   peo-ple
last   saw   you laugh-ing.   If   this   world makes you   craz-y   and you're

Original key: F♯ major. This edition has been transposed down one half-step to be more playable.

true col - ors are beau - ti - ful, ooh, __ like a rain - bow.

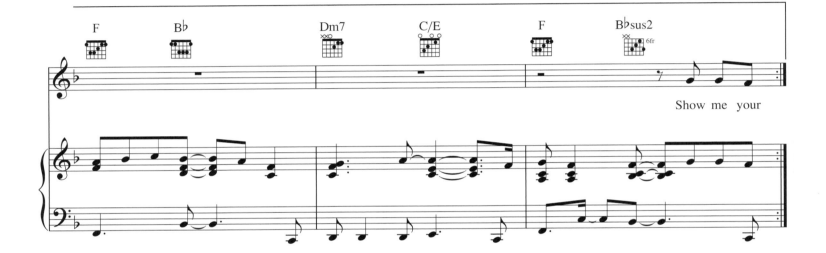

Show me your

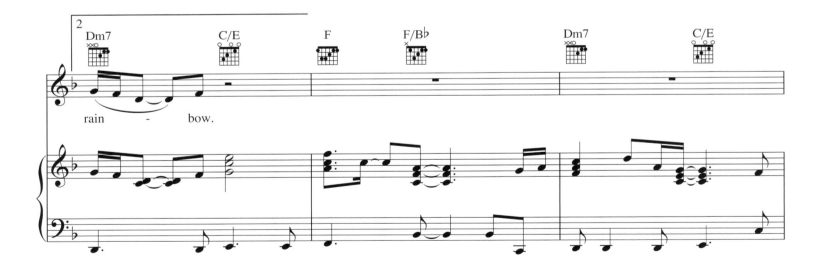

rain - bow.

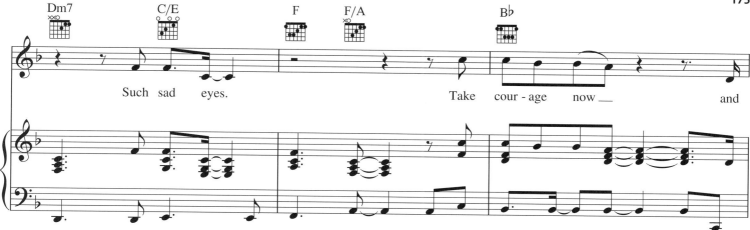

Such sad eyes. Take cour-age now ___ and

re - al - ize. When this world makes you craz - y and you're

tak - in' all you can bear, ___ just call me up be-cause you know I'll be there. And I see your

D.S. al Coda

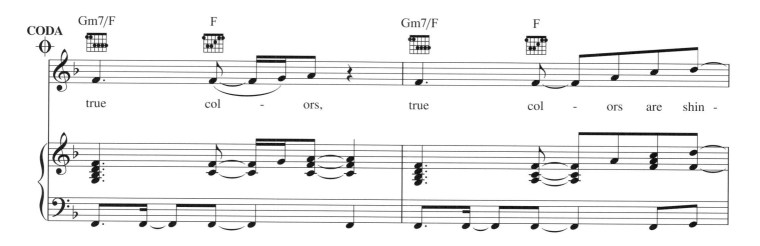

CODA

true col - ors, true col - ors are shin -

-in' through. I see your true col - ors and

that's why I love ___ you. So, don't be a-fraid, ___ just

let them ___ show. ___ Your true col - ors,

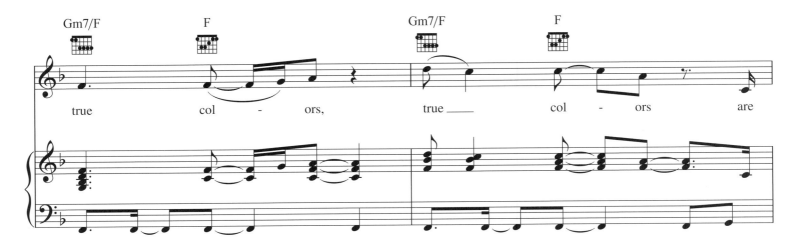

true col - ors, true ___ col - ors are

beau - ti - ful, beau - ti - ful like a rain - bow.

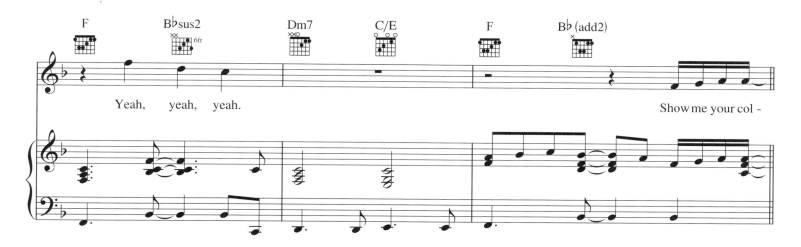

Yeah, yeah, yeah. Show me your col -

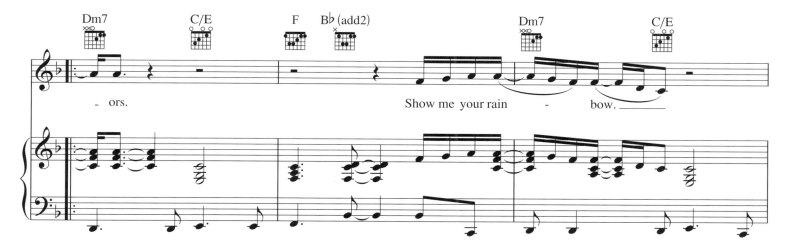

- ors. Show me your rain - bow. _____

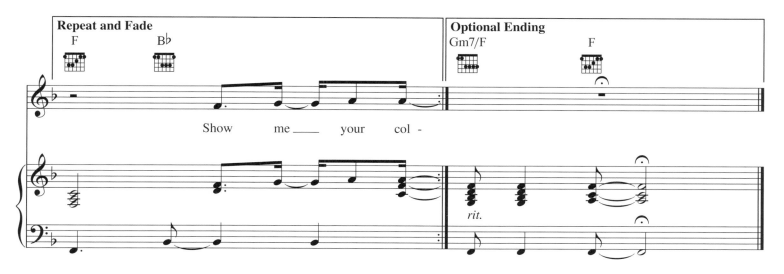

Repeat and Fade

Show me ___ your col -

Optional Ending

rit.

WE ARE FAMILY

Words and Music by NILE RODGERS
and BERNARD EDWARDS

we're giv-ing love like a fam-'ly does, oh, ___ yeah. We are fam-i-ly;

(We are fam - i - ly;) I got all my sis-ters with me.

(I got all my sis-ters with me.) We are fam - i - ly; (We are fam - i - ly.) ___

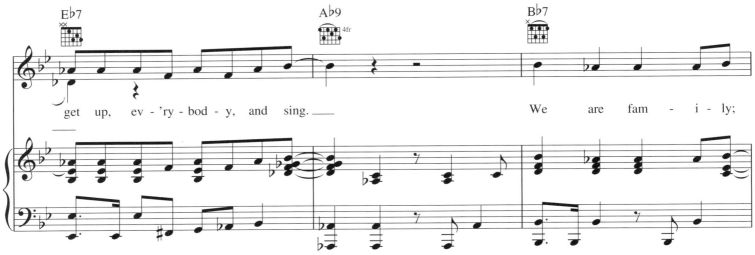

get up, ev-'ry-bod-y, and sing. ___ We are fam - i - ly;

(We are fam - i - ly.) I got all my sis - ters with me.

(I got all my sis - ters with me.) We are fam - i - ly; (Fam - i - ly.) __

To Coda get up, ev - 'ry - bod - y, and sing. __ Liv - ing life is fun, and we've just

be - gun to get our share __ of this world's __

you do, you won't go wrong, __ oh no. This is our fam - 'ly jewel, yeah, __ yeah. ____

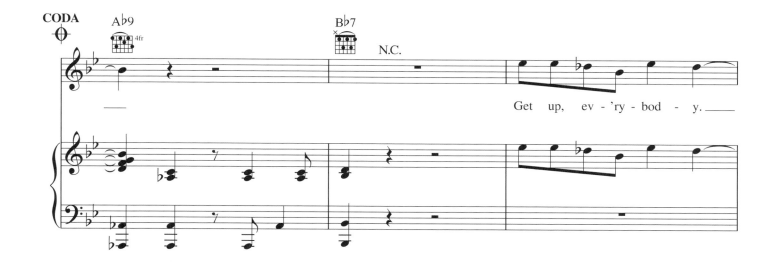

____ Get up, ev - 'ry - bod - y. ____

____ Jump! Here we go.

We are fam - i - ly;
(We are fam - i - ly;)

I got all my sis - ters with me.
(I got all my sis - ters.)
We are fam - i - ly;

get up, ev - 'ry - bod - y, and sing.

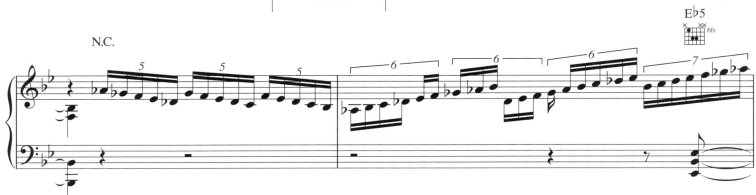

WE ARE THE WORLD

Words and Music by LIONEL RICHIE
and MICHAEL JACKSON

Moderately slow

_to make a bright - er day, _ so let's _ start giv - ing._ There's a

choice we're mak - ing, _____ we're sav - ing our _ own lives, _ it's true; _

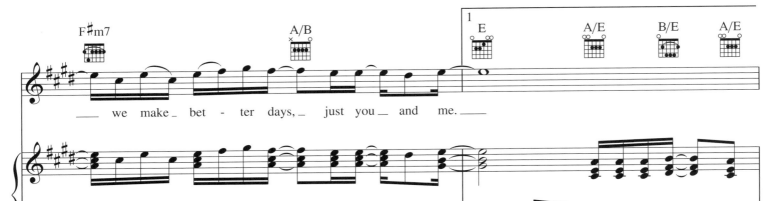

_ we make _ bet - ter days, _ just you _ and me. _

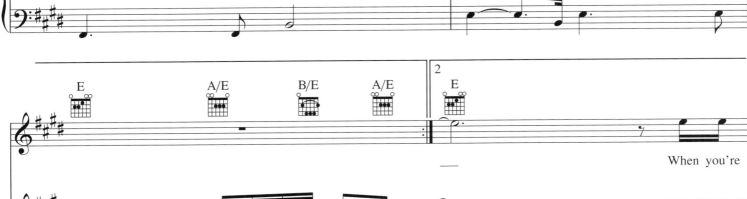

_ When you're

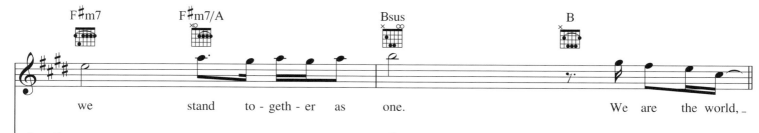

we are the chil - dren, we are the ones

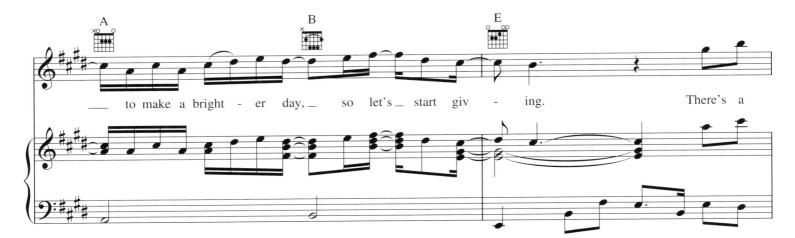

to make a bright - er day, so let's start giv - ing. There's a

choice we're mak - ing, we're sav - ing our own lives, it's true;

we make bet - ter days, just you and me. We are the world,

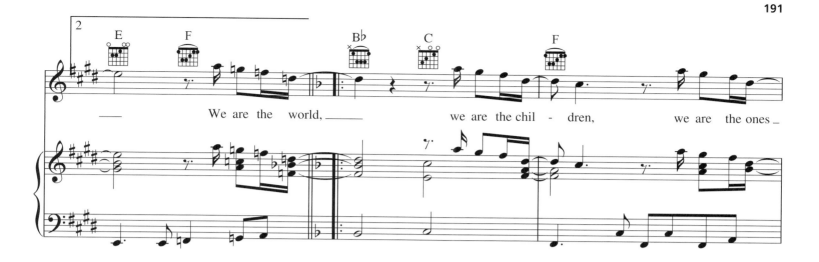

We are the world, _____ we are the chil - dren, we are the ones _

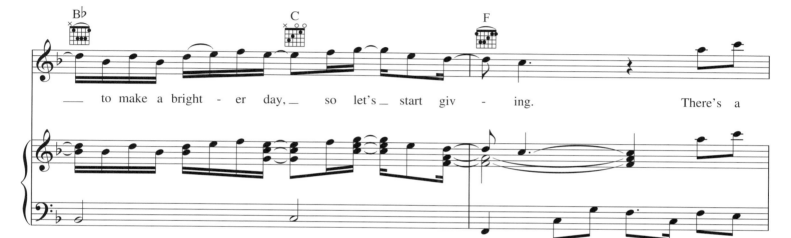

_ to make a bright - er day, _ so let's _ start giv - ing. There's a

choice we're mak - ing, _____ we're sav - ing our _ own lives, _ it's true; _

Repeat and Fade

_ we make _ bet - ter days, _ just you _ and me. ____ We are the world, _

WE'RE ALL IN THIS TOGETHER

from the Disney Channel Original Movie HIGH SCHOOL MUSICAL

Words and Music by MATTHEW GERRARD
and ROBBIE NEVIL

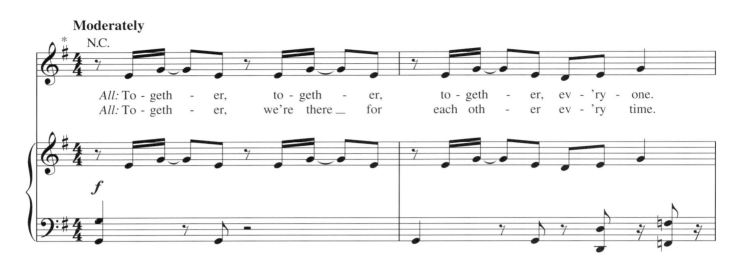

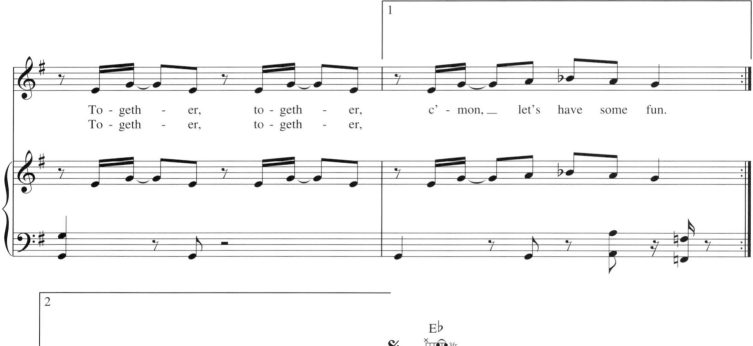

*Recorded a half step lower.

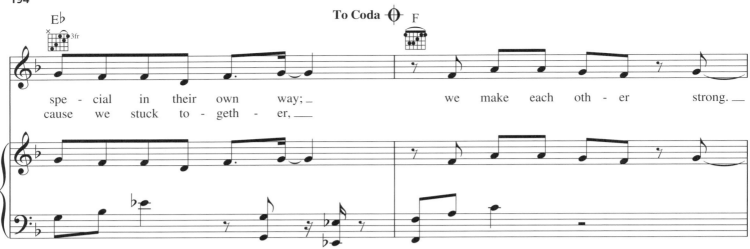

special in their own way; ___ we make each oth - er strong. ___
cause we stuck to - geth - er, ___

___ We're not the same; ___ we're dif - f'rent in a good way. ___

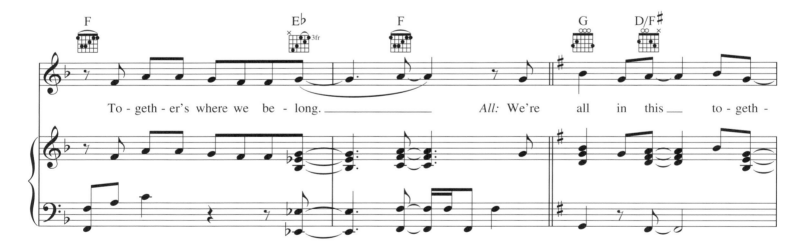

To - geth - er's where we be - long. _____ *All:* We're all in this ___ to - geth -

- er; once ___ we know that we are, we're all stars, and we see ___ that. We're

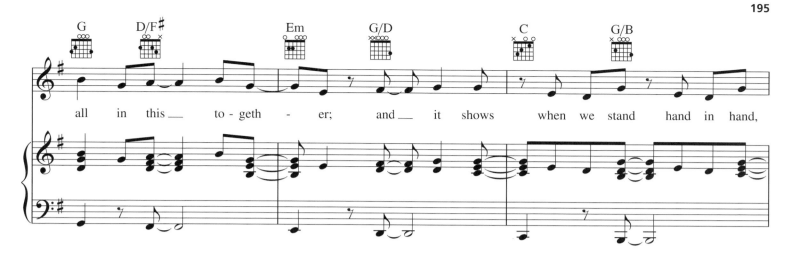

all in this __ to - geth - er; and __ it shows when we stand hand in hand,

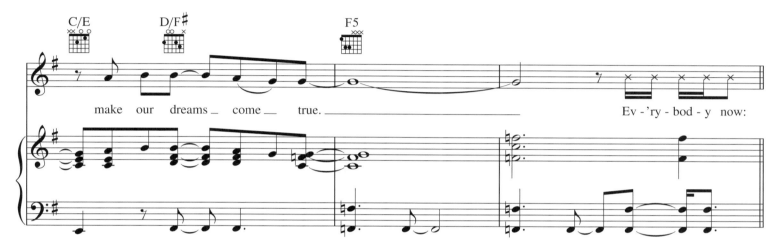

make our dreams __ come __ true. _____ Ev - 'ry - bod - y now:

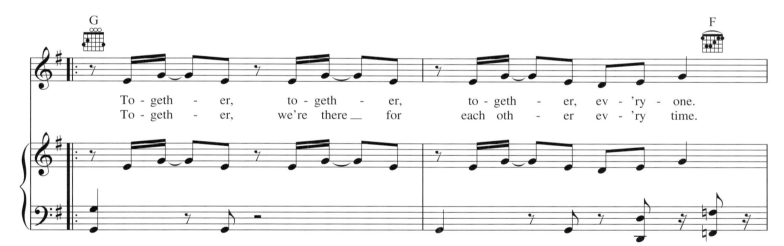

To - geth - er, to - geth - er, to - geth - er, ev - 'ry - one.
To - geth - er, we're there __ for each oth - er ev - 'ry time.

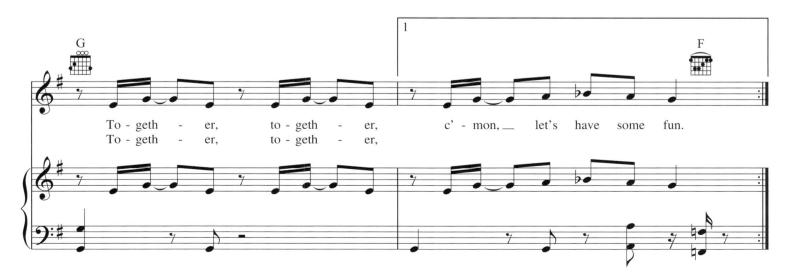

To - geth - er, to - geth - er, c' - mon, __ let's have some fun.
To - geth - er, to - geth - er,

D.S. al Coda

c'- mon, __ let's do this right.

CODA

cham - pi - ons one and all. __

All: We're all in this __ to - geth - er; once __ we know
all in this __ to - geth - er; when __ we reach,

that we are, we're all stars, and we see __ that. We're all in this __ to - geth -
we can fly, know in - side we can make __ it. We're all in this __ to - geth -

- er; and __ it shows when we stand hand in hand, make our dreams __ come... We're
- er; once __ we see there's a chance that we have

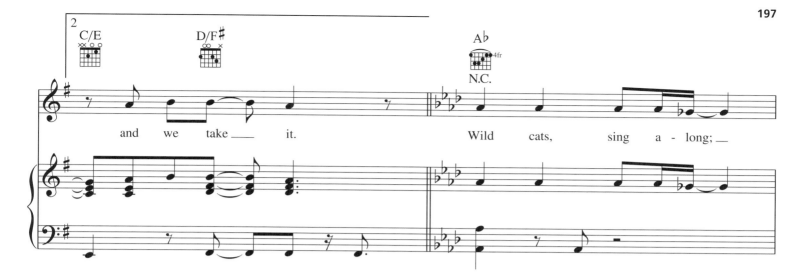

and we take ___ it. Wild cats, sing a - long; ___

yeah, you real - ly got it go - in' on. ___ Wild cats in the house; ___

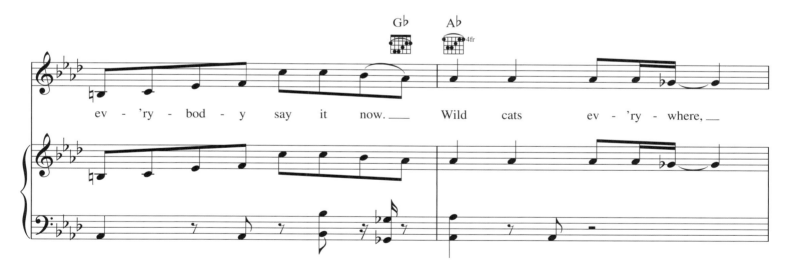

ev - 'ry - bod - y say it now. ___ Wild cats ev - 'ry - where, ___

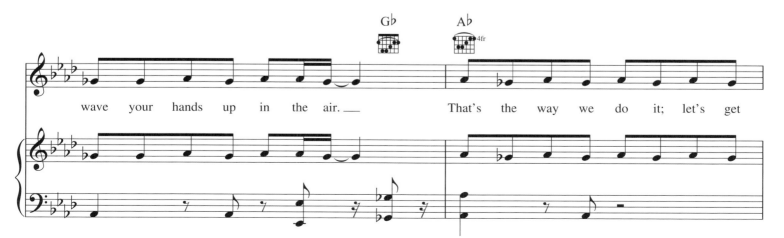

wave your hands up in the air. ___ That's the way we do it; let's get

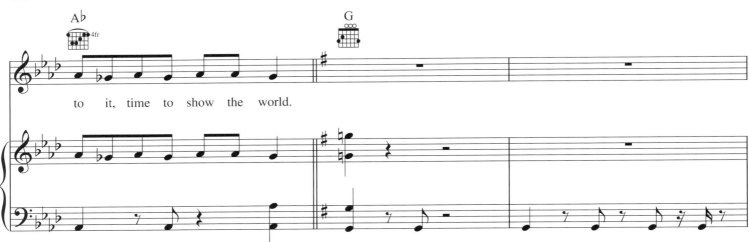

to it, time to show the world.

Hey. ___

Oh. ___   Hey, ___   oh, _____   al - right, here we go. We're

all in this ___ to - geth - er;   once ___ we know   that we are,   we're all stars,
all in this ___ to - geth - er;   when ___ we reach,   we can fly,   know in - side

and we see ___ that. We're all in this ___ to-geth - er; and ___ it shows
we can make ___ it. We're all in this ___ to-geth - er; once ___ we see

when we stand hand in hand, make our dreams ___ come... We're
there's a chance that we have, and we take ___ it.

Wild cats ev - 'ry - where, ___ wave your hands up in the air. ___

That's the way we do it; let's get to it, c' - mon ___ ev - 'ry - one! _____

WHAT A WONDERFUL WORLD

Words and Music by GEORGE DAVID WEISS
and BOB THIELE

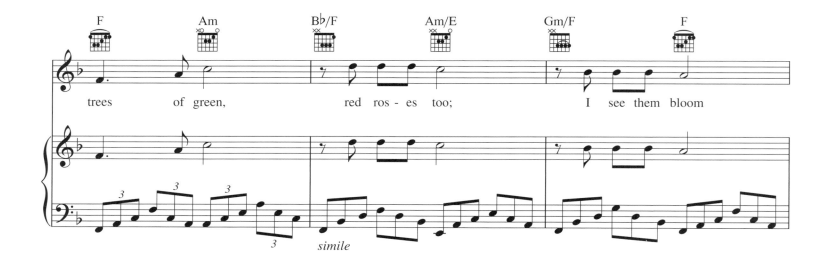

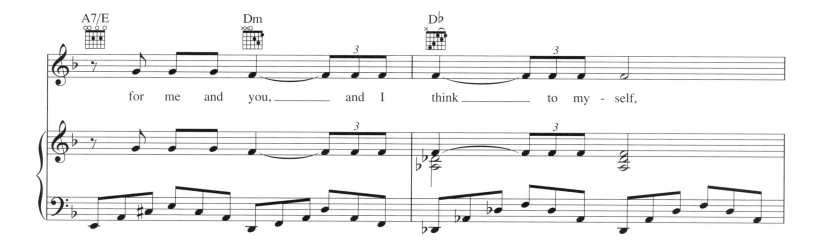

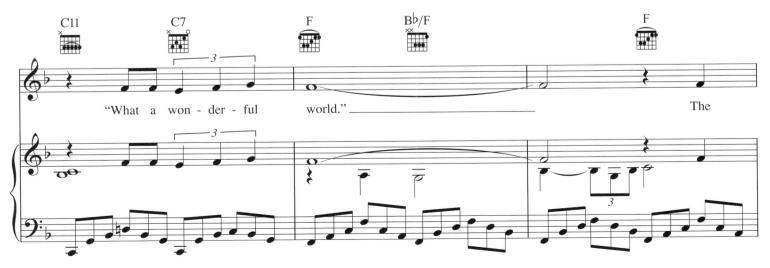

col - ors of the rain - bow, so pret - ty in the sky, are

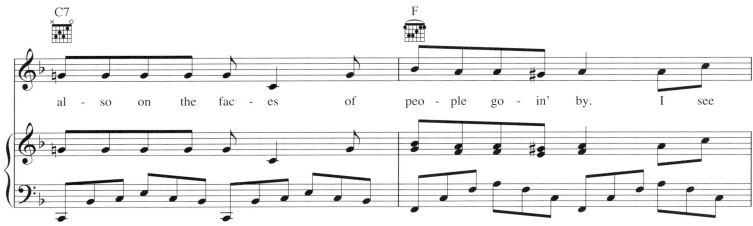

al - so on the fac - es of peo - ple go - in' by. I see

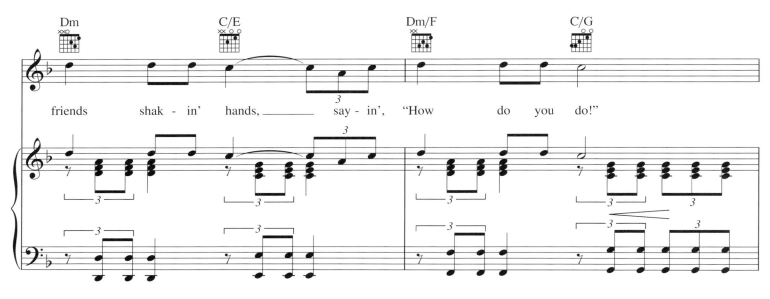

friends shak - in' hands, _____ say - in', "How do you do!"

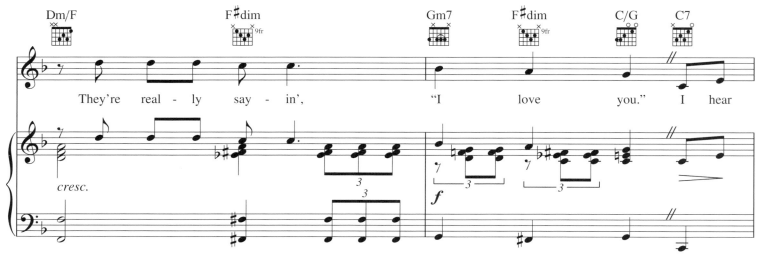

They're real - ly say - in', "I love you." I hear

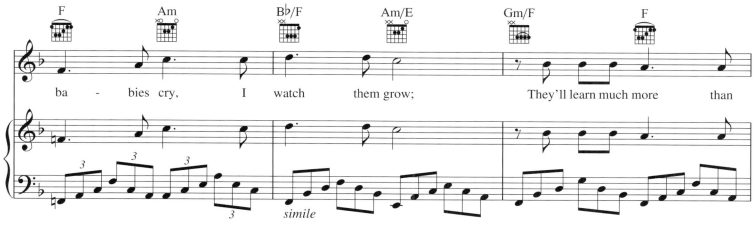

ba - bies cry, I watch them grow; They'll learn much more than

I'll ___ ev-er know, ___ and I think ___ to my-self, "What a won-der-ful

Rubato

world." _____ Yes, I think to my-self,

"What a won-der-ful world." _____

rit.

TOP OF THE WORLD

Words and Music by JOHN BETTIS
and RICHARD CARPENTER

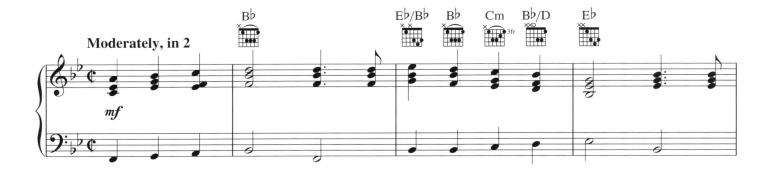

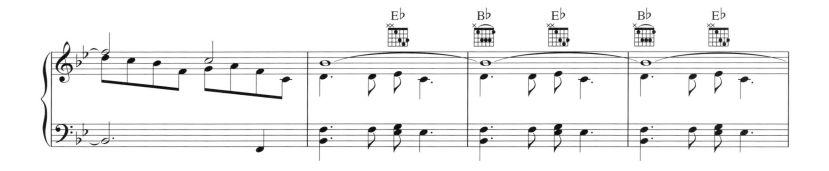

Such a feel-in's com-in' o - ver me.
Some-thing in ___ the wind has learned ___ my name.

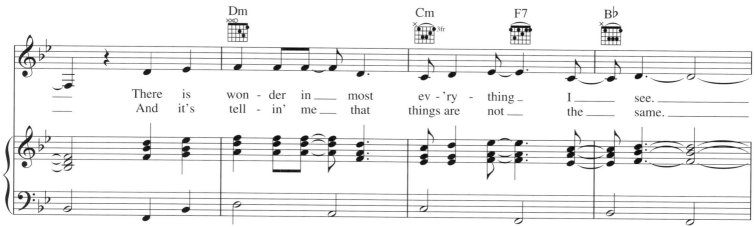

There is won-der in ___ most ev-'ry - thing ___ I ___ see. ___
And it's tell - in' me ___ that things are not ___ the ___ same. ___

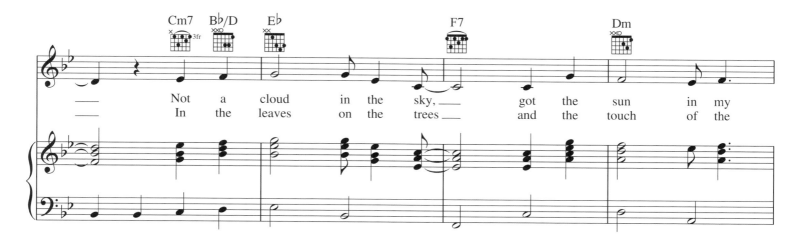

Not a cloud in the sky, ___ got the sun in my
In the cloud leaves on the trees ___ and the sun touch of the

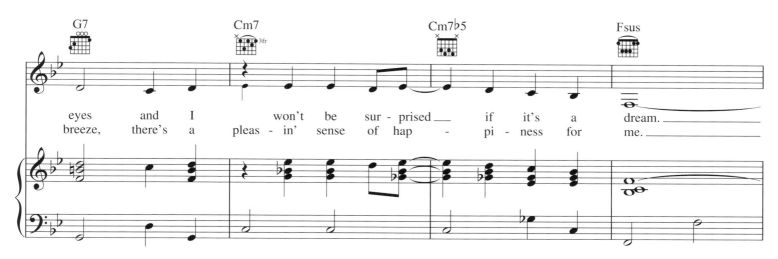

eyes and I won't be sur - prised ___ if it's a dream. ___
breeze, there's a pleas - in' sense of hap - pi - ness for me. ___

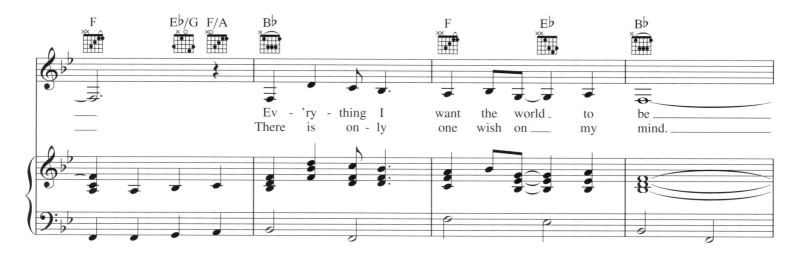

Ev - 'ry - thing I want the world to be ___
There is on - ly one wish on ___ my mind. ___

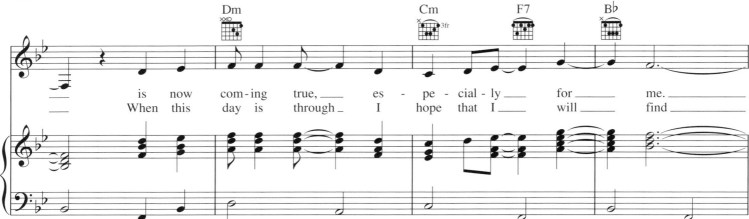

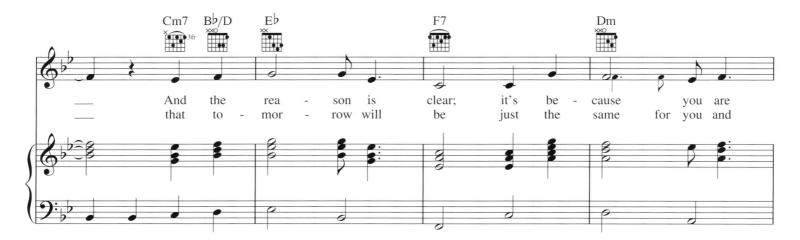

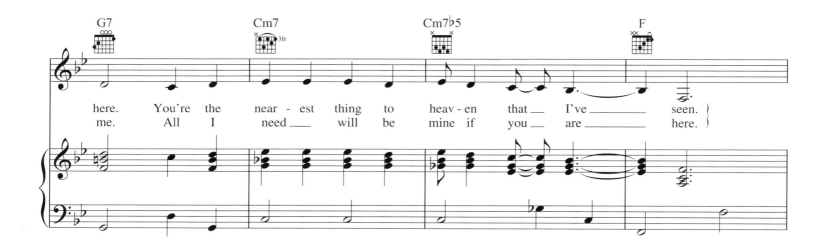

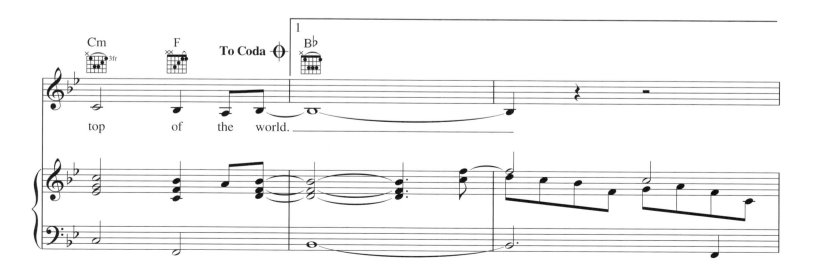

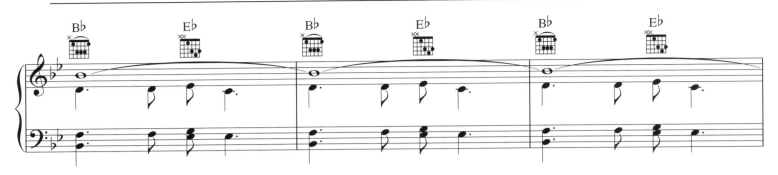

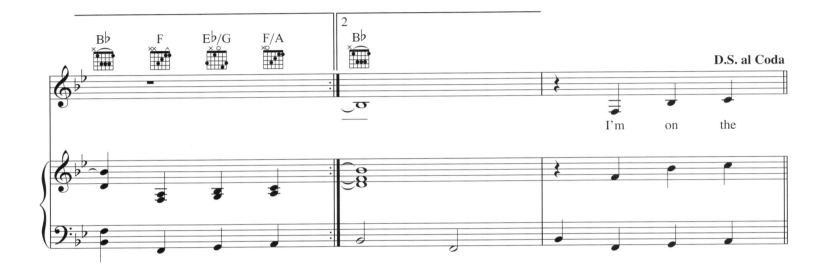

I'm   on   the

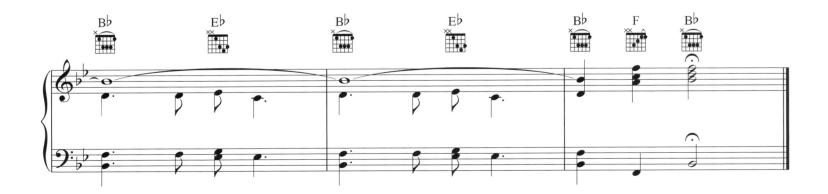

WHAT THE WORLD NEEDS NOW IS LOVE

Lyric by HAL DAVID
Music by BURT BACHARACH

With a Jazz Waltz feel

world needs now is love, sweet love.

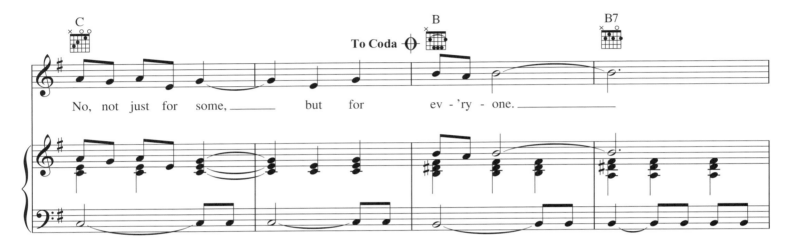

No, not just for some, _____ but for ev-'ry-one. _____

To Coda

Lord, we don't need an-oth-er moun-tain. _____ There are
Lord, we don't need an-oth-er mead-ow. _____ There are

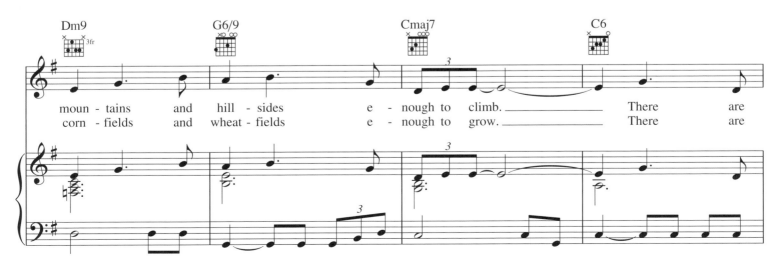

moun-tains and hill-sides e-nough to climb. _____ There are
corn-fields and wheat-fields e-nough to grow. _____ There are

o - ceans and riv - ers e - nough to cross, _____ e - nough to last ____
sun - beams and moon - beams e - nough to shine, _____ oh, lis - ten, Lord, __

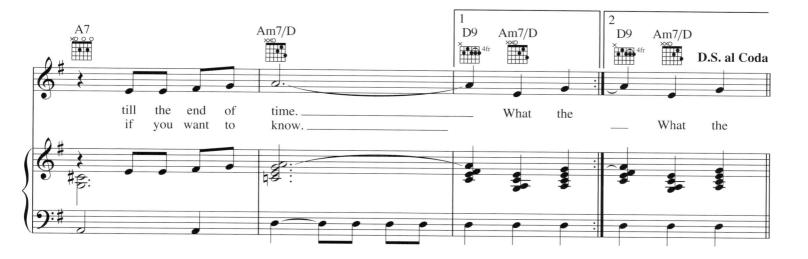

till the end of time. _____ What the
if you want to know. _____ __ What the

D.S. al Coda

ev - 'ry - one. _____ No, not just for some, _____ oh, but

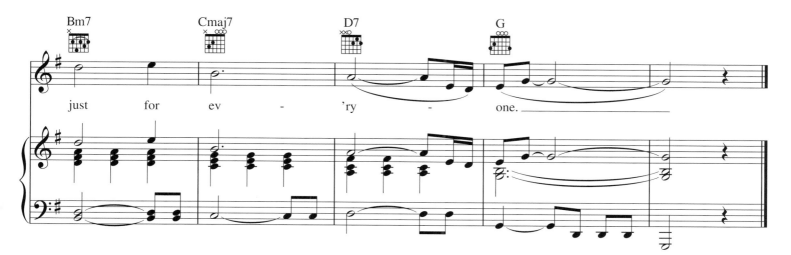

just for ev - 'ry - one. _____

WITH YOU I'M BORN AGAIN

Words by CAROL CONNORS
Music by DAVID SHIRE

YOU'LL BE IN MY HEART

(Pop Version)

from Walt Disney Pictures' TARZAN™

Words and Music by
PHIL COLLINS

Moderately

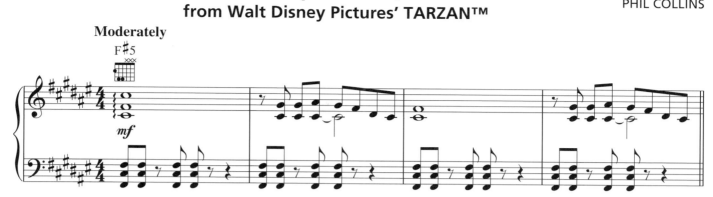

Come stop your cry-ing; __ it will be all right. Just take my hand,

hold it tight. _____ I will pro-tect you from all a-round __ you.

I will be here; don't you __ cry.

For one so small you
Why can't they un-der-stand the

seem so ___ strong. ___ / My arms will hold you, ___ keep you
way we ___ feel? ___ They just don't trust ___ what they

safe and ___ warm. ___ This bond be - tween us
can't ex - plain. ___ I know we're dif - f'rent, but

can't be bro - ken. I will be here; don't you ___ cry. 'Cause
deep in - side ___ us we're not that dif - fer - ent at all. ___ And

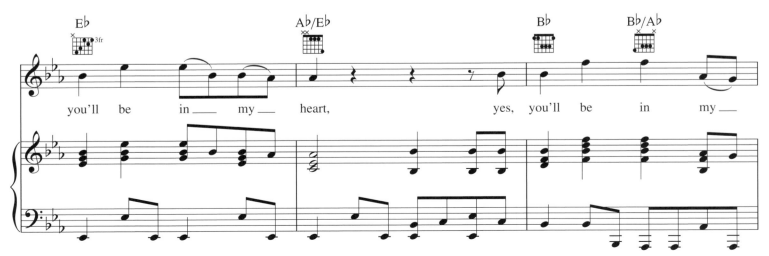

you'll be in ___ my ___ heart, yes, you'll be in my ___

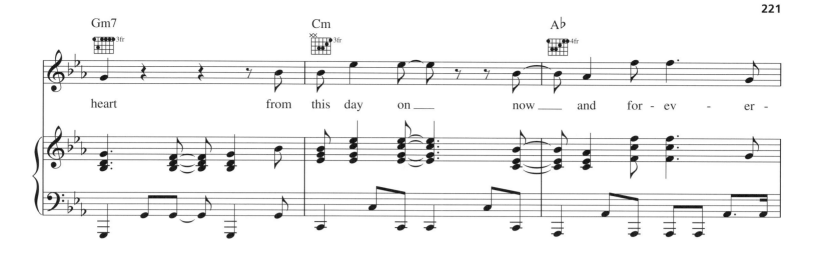

heart   from this day on ___ now ___ and for-ev-er-

more.   You'll   be   in ___ my ___

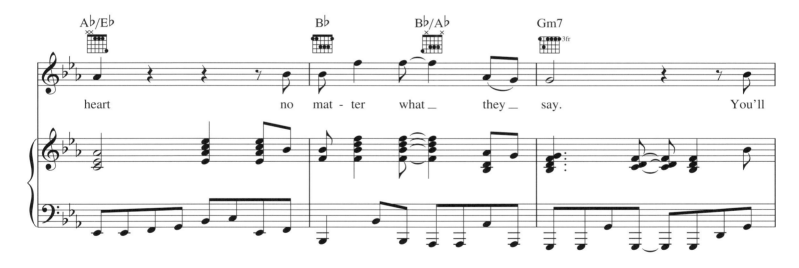

heart   no mat-ter what ___ they ___ say.   You'll

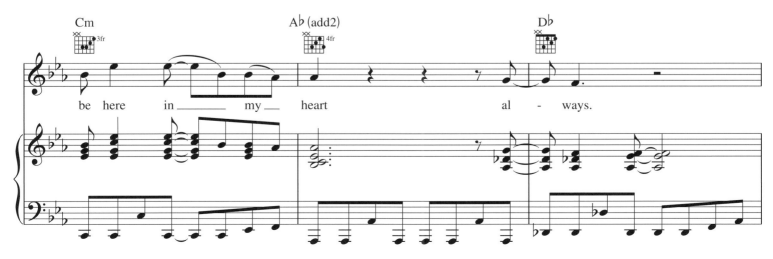

be here in ___ my ___ heart   al - ways.

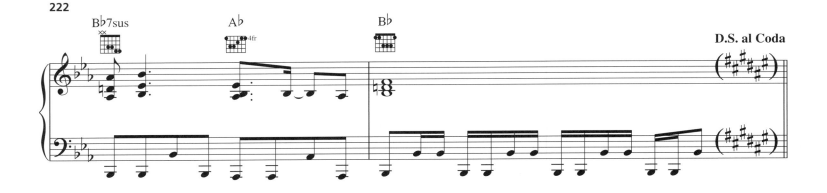

D.S. al Coda

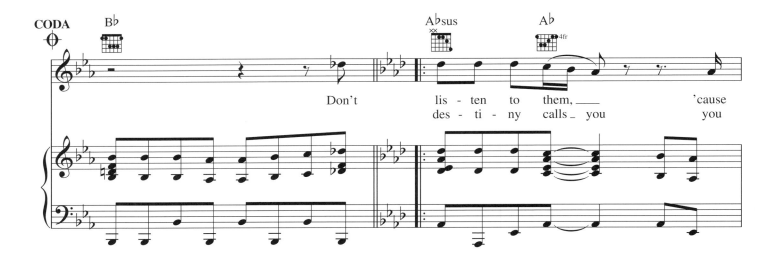

CODA

Don't lis - ten to them, ____ 'cause
des - ti - ny calls _ you you

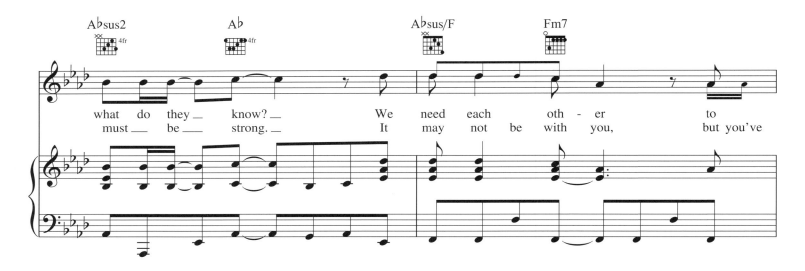

what do they _ know? _ We need each oth - er, to
must _ be _ strong. _ It may not be with you, but you've

have, to _ hold. _ }
got to hold _ on. _ } They'll _ see _ in time, I ____

show them ___ to-geth - er, ___'cause   you'll be   in ___ my ___ heart.   Be - lieve me,

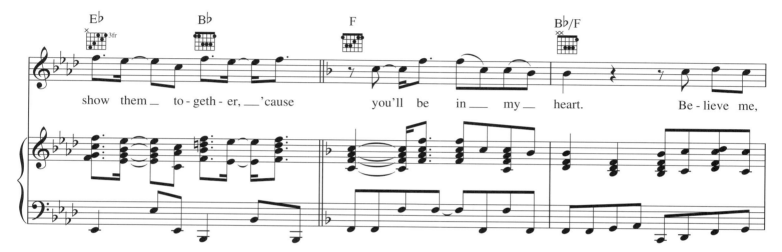

you'll   be   in ___   my ___ heart.   I'll be there from this   day   on, ___   now ___

___ and   for - ev - er - more. ___

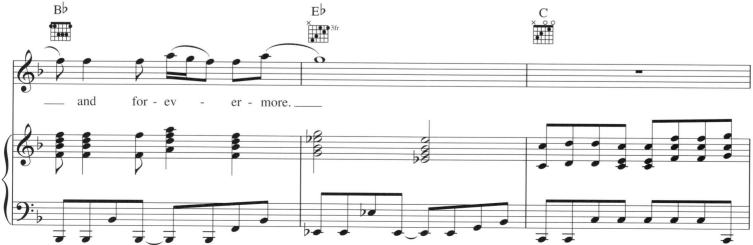

there for _ you al - ways, al - ways _ and al - ways. _

Just look o - ver your shoul - der. Just look o -

- ver your shoul - der. Just look o - ver your shoul - der;

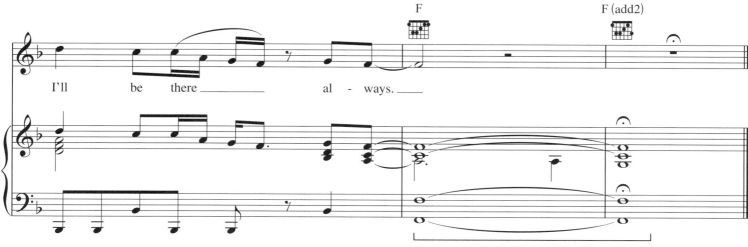

I'll be there _ al - ways. _

YOU RAISE ME UP

Words and Music by BRENDAN GRAHAM
and ROLF LOVLAND

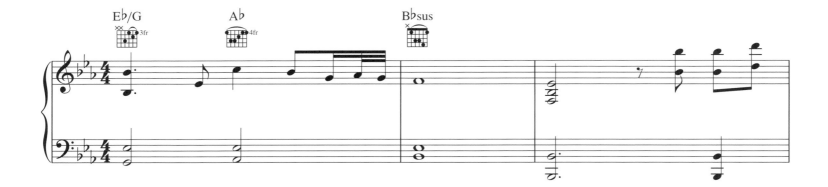

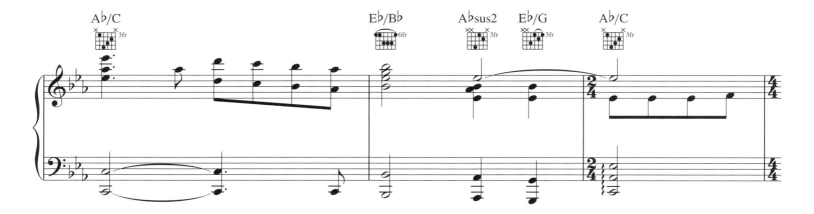

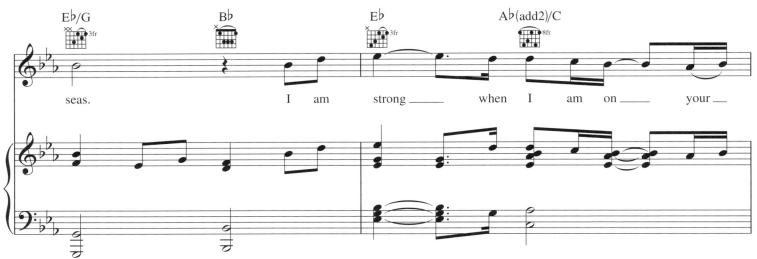

seas.   I am strong _____ when I am on _____ your _____

shoul - ders. ____ You raise me up   to more than I ___ can be.

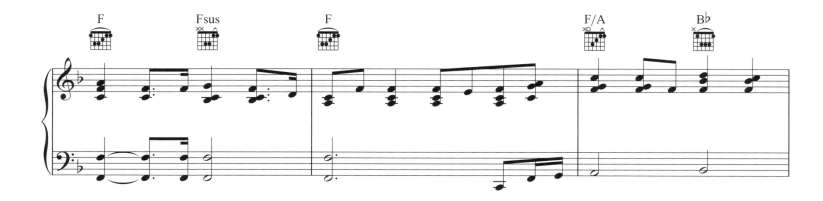

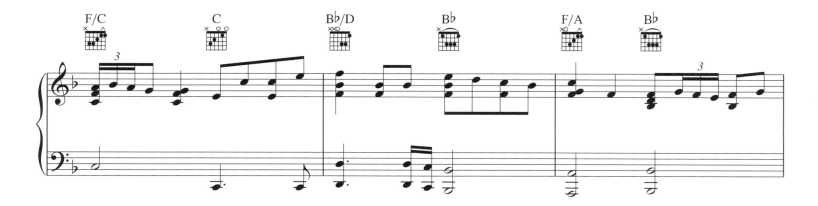

You raise me up so I can stand on

moun - tains. You raise me up to walk on storm - y

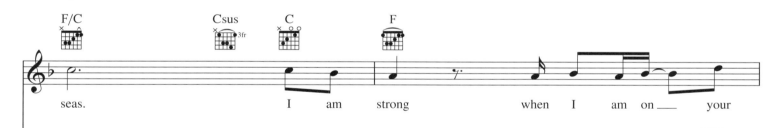

seas. I am strong when I am on _____ your

shoul - ders. You raise me up to more than I _____ can _____

be.

You raise me up so I can stand on

moun - tains. You raise me up to walk on storm - y

seas. I _____ am ___ strong _____ when I am on ___ your

shoul - ders. You raise me up to more than I _____ can

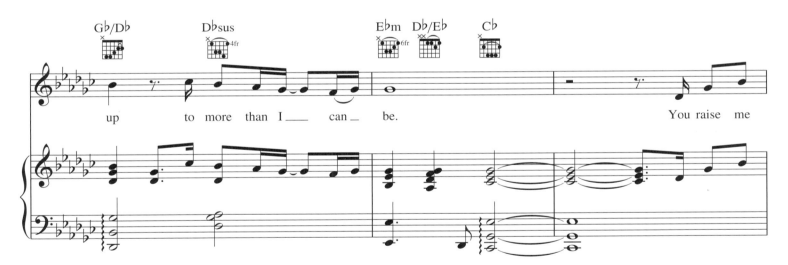

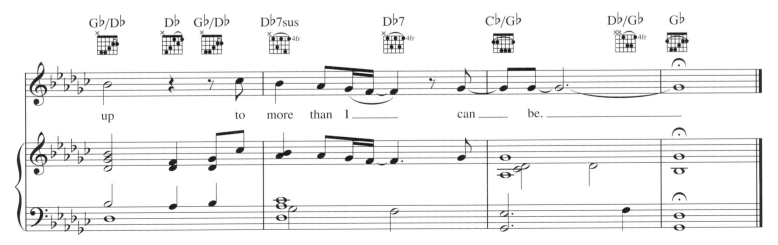

YOU'VE GOT A FRIEND

Words and Music by
CAROLE KING

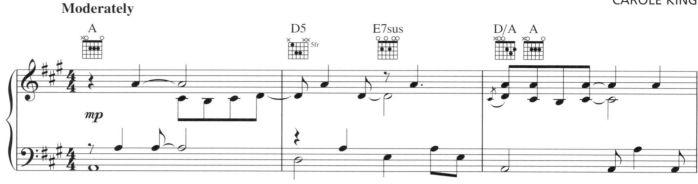

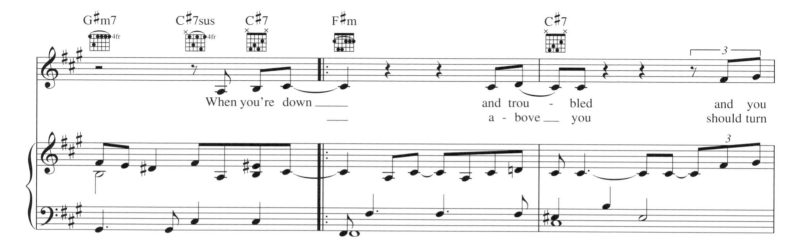

close your eyes __ and think of me __ and soon I will __ be __ there __
keep your head __ to-geth __ - er __ and call my name _____ out

__ loud, _____ now; __ to bright-en up __ e - ven your dark - est night. __
soon I'll be knock - ing up - on __ your door. __

You just call _____ out my name, __

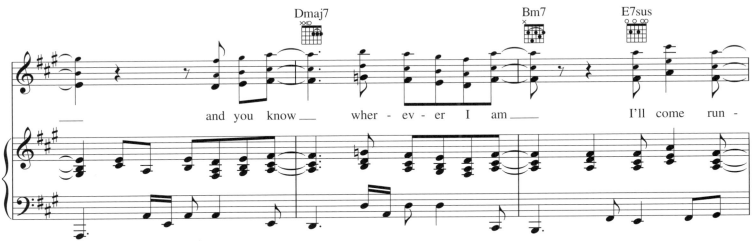

__ and you know __ wher - ev - er I am _____ I'll come run -

*Vocal harmony sung 2nd time only

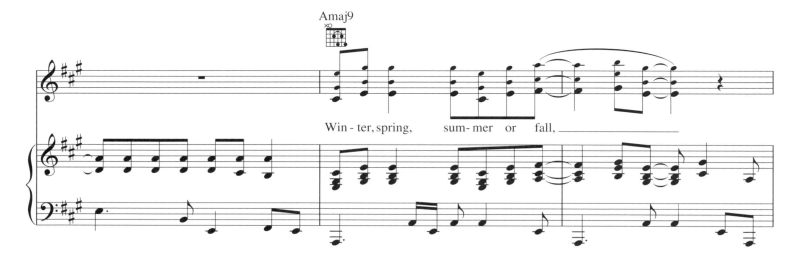

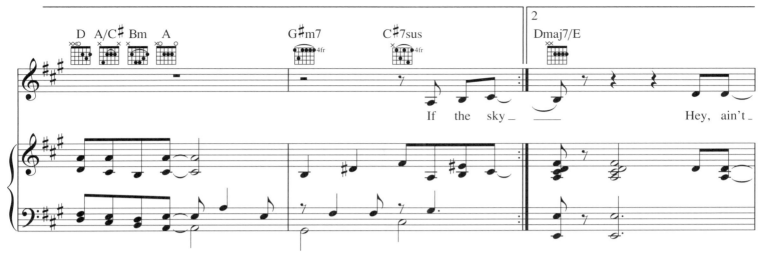

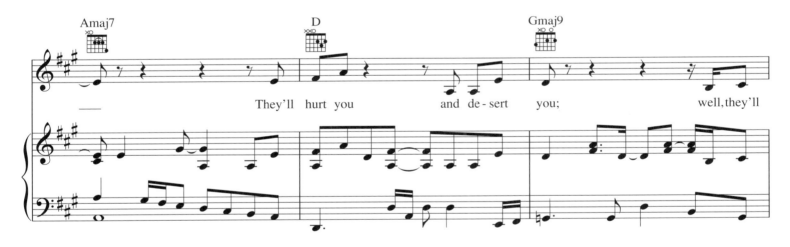

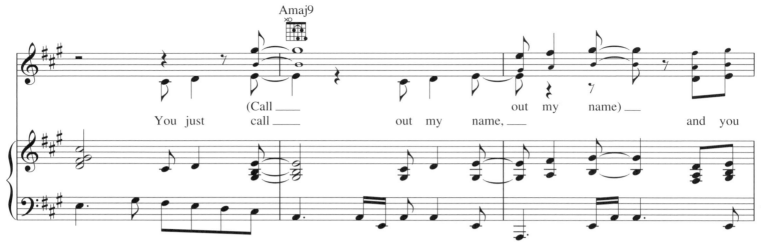

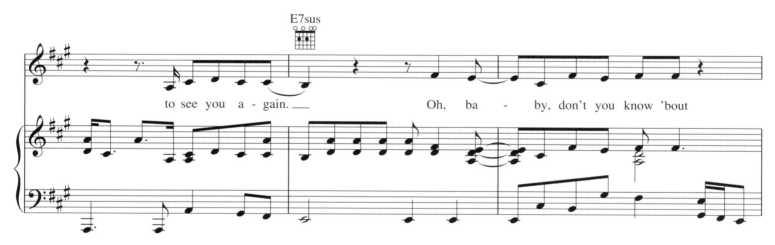

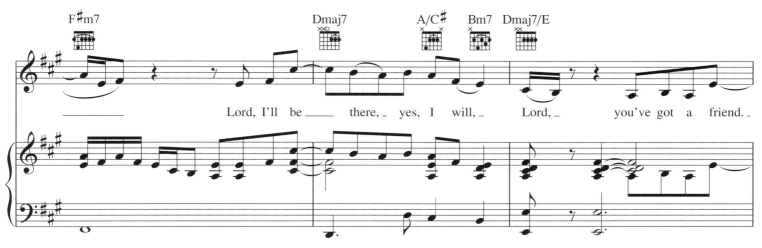

Lord, I'll be __ there, _ yes, I will, _ Lord, _ you've got a friend. _

You've _ got a friend, _ yeah.

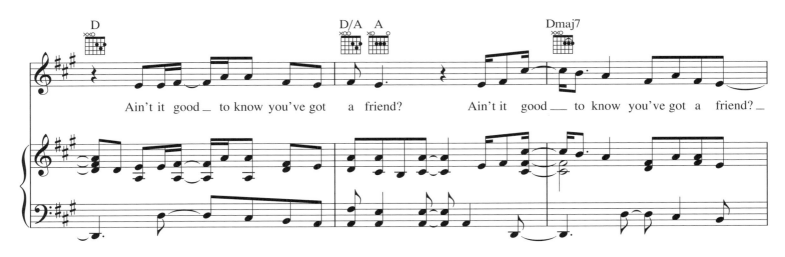

Ain't it good _ to know you've got a friend? Ain't it good __ to know you've got a friend? _

Oh, yeah, __ yeah, you've got a friend. __

The Finest Inspirational Music
Songbooks arranged for piano, voice, and guitar.

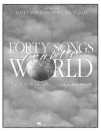

40 SONGS FOR A BETTER WORLD

40 songs with a message, including: All You Need Is Love • Bless the Beasts and Children • Colors of the Wind • Everything Is Beautiful • He Ain't Heavy...He's My Brother • I Am Your Child • Love Can Build a Bridge • What a Wonderful World • What the World Needs Now Is Love • You've Got a Friend • more.
00310096 ....$15.95

THE BEST PRAISE & WORSHIP SONGS EVER

80 all-time favorites: Awesome God • Breathe • Days of Elijah • Here I Am to Worship • I Could Sing of Your Love Forever • Open the Eyes of My Heart • Shout to the Lord • We Bow Down • dozens more.
00311057 ....$19.95

THE BIG BOOK OF CONTEMPORARY CHRISTIAN FAVORITES

50 of today's top CCM hits: Always Have, Always Will • Angels • El Shaddai • Find a Way • Friends • The Great Divide • I Will Be Here • I'll Lead You Home • Jesus Freak • Let Us Pray • Love in Any Language • A Maze of Grace • People Need the Lord • Pray • Shine on Us • Speechless • This Love • Thy Word • To Know You • Undivided • Via Dolorosa • Whatever You Ask • Where There Is Faith • Wisdom • and more.
00310021 ....$19.95

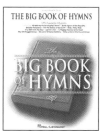

THE BIG BOOK OF HYMNS

An invaluable collection of 125 favorite hymns, including: All Hail the Power of Jesus' Name • Battle Hymn of the Republic • Blessed Assurance • For the Beauty of the Earth • Holy, Holy, Holy • It Is Well with My Soul • Just as I Am • A Mighty Fortress Is Our God • The Old Rugged Cross • Onward Christian Soldiers • Rock of Ages • Sweet By and By • What a Friend We Have in Jesus • Wondrous Love • and more.
00310510 ....$17.95

For More Information, See Your Local Music Dealer, Or Write To:

7777 W. Bluemound Rd. P.O. Box 13819 Milwaukee, WI 53213

Visit us at www.halleonard.com for complete songlists and our entire catalog of titles.

Prices, contents, and availability subject to change without notice. Some products may not be available outside the U.S.A.

CHRISTIAN CHILDREN'S SONGBOOK

101 songs from Sunday School, including: Awesome God • The B-I-B-L-E • The Bible Tells Me So • Clap Your Hands • Day by Day • He's Got the Whole World in His Hands • I Am a C-H-R-I-S-T-I-A-N • I'm in the Lord's Army • If You're Happy (And You Know It) • Jesus Loves Me • Kum Ba Yah • Let There Be Peace on Earth • This Little Light of Mine • When the Saints Go Marching In • and more.
00310472 ....$19.95

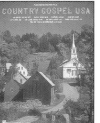

COUNTRY/GOSPEL U.S.A.

50 songs written for piano/guitar/four-part vocal. Highlights: An American Trilogy • Daddy Sang Bass • He Set Me Free • I Saw the Light • I'll Meet You in the Morning • Kum Ba Yah • Mansion Over the Hilltop • Love Lifted Me • Turn Your Radio On • When the Saints Go Marching In • many more.
00240139 ....$10.95

FAVORITE HYMNS

71 all-time favorites, including: Amazing Grace • Ave Maria • Christ the Lord Is Risen Today • Crown Him with Many Crowns • Faith of Our Fathers • He's Got the Whole World in His Hands • In the Sweet By and By • Jesus Loves Me! • Just a Closer Walk With Thee • Kum Ba Yah • A Mighty Fortress Is Our God • Onward Christian Soldiers • Rock of Ages • Swing Low, Sweet Chariot • Were You There? • and many more.
00490436 ....$12.95

HE IS EXALTED

Music for Blended Worship
52 beloved hymns and choruses: Awesome God • How Great Thou Art • Lord, I Lift Your Name on High • O Worship the King • Shout to the Lord • The Wonderful Cross • more!
00311068 ....$14.95

I COULD SING OF YOUR LOVE FOREVER

Some of today's most popular CCM artists and their songs are included in this matching folio. Songs: Did You Feel the Mountains Tremble? (Matt Redman) • The Happy Song (Delirious?) • I Could Sing of Your Love Forever (Sonicflood) • Open the Eyes of My Heart (Praise Band) • Pour Out Your Spirit (Tom Lane) • Trading My Sorrows (Darrell Evans) • You Are Merciful to Me (Ian White) • and more.
00306380 ....$14.95

OUR GOD REIGNS

A collection of over 70 songs of praise and worship, including: El Shaddai • Find Us Faithful • His Eyes • Holy Ground • How Majestic Is Your Name • Proclaim the Glory of the Lord • Sing Your Praise to the Lord • Thy Word • and more.
00311695 ....$17.95

SONGS FROM PASSION

This great collection features 14 songs from the recordings *Better Is One Day* and *Live Worship from the 268 Generation*. Includes: Be Glorified • Every Move I Make • Freedom Song • The Heart of Worship • I Will Exalt Your Name • I've Found Jesus • We Fall Down • You Alone • You Are My King • more.
00306345 ....$12.95

TOP CHRISTIAN HITS OF 2003-2004

Your favorites by Avalon, Audio Adrenaline, MercyMe, Stacie Orrico, Third Day and many others! Includes: All About Love • Different Kind of Free • Everything to Me • God of All • Holy • I Can Only Imagine • I Still Believe • I Thank You • It Is You • Legacy • Meant to Live • Pray • Say It Loud • Show Me Your Glory • more.
00311102 ....$14.95

TRADITIONAL GOSPEL

21 songs, including: His Eye Is On The Sparrow • How Great Thou Art • Just a Closer Walk with Thee • The Old Rugged Cross • Peace in the Valley • Take My Hand, Precious Lord.

00361361 ....$8.95

ULTIMATE GOSPEL – 100 SONGS OF DEVOTION

An impressive collection of 100 Gospel favorites, including: El Shaddai • His Eye Is on the Sparrow • How Great Thou Art • Just a Closer Walk with Thee • Lead Me, Guide Me • (There'll Be) Peace in the Valley (For Me) • Precious Lord, Take My Hand • Wings of a Dove • more.
00241009 ....$19.95

0606